Loving Correction

Loving Correction

An Exegetical Commentary on First Corinthians Sixteen

By
Spiros Zodhiates, Th.D.

AMG
PUBLISHERS
Chattanooga, TN 37422

Loving Correction

An Exegetical Commentary on First Corinthians Sixteen

ISBN 0-89957-477-7

Printed in the United States of America
02 01 00 99 98 97 –R– 7 6 5 4 3 2 1

To Paul Jenks,
whose life exemplifies the admonition
of the Apostle Paul to correct one another in love.

Contents

Preface

Paul had lived an exemplary life among the Corinthians for eighteen months, but he observed much in their lives that needed to be corrected. His first epistle to them, after he departed to Ephesus, was to summarize areas which needed correction.

We find in the two closing verses of the 16th chapter reminders of the grace of the Lord Jesus Christ and of Paul's own love for the Corinthians. Paul wanted them to remember these things.

These two verses prompted the title of this book, *Loving Correction.* Whenever the need for correction is observed, the Christian should never hesitate to provide it, but always do so in the love of Christ.

For your convenience, we have referenced the Greek words cited in this work to Strong's *Greek Dictionary of the New Testament.*

Spiros Zodhiates

An Overview of First Corinthians

Author: Paul the Apostle, author of thirteen other epistles to various individuals and congregations.

Date: About A.D. 55.

Recipients: The congregation Paul had established in Corinth.

Place: From Ephesus

Theme: Paul had received news about the Corinthian brethren from several sources (1 Cor. 1:11; 7:1; 16:17). The church was afflicted with many of the problems that face young churches and new converts. The Apostle, under the inspiration of the Holy Spirit, decided to write this urgent letter to admonish and instruct the church. Among other topics he discussed: the necessity of church discipline (5:1–13); divisions and disputes among Christians (1:10–16; 6:1–11); matters of conscience (8:1–13; 10:19–33); the support of preachers (9:1–27); abuses of the Lord's Supper (10:16–17, 21; 11:17–34); the misuse of spiritual gifts (12:1—14:40); and the importance of the resurrection of Jesus Christ (15:1–58).

An Outline of First Corinthians

In the days of the Apostle Paul, Corinth was the capital city of the Roman province of Achaia and the glory of Greece. Though its great ancient splendor had been destroyed by the Romans in 120 B.C., the city was rebuilt under Julius Caesar and restored to wealth and luxury under Augustus. Among all the cities of the world, however, it was most well-known for its lewdness. The Apostle Paul lived in Corinth for eighteen months (Acts 18:11). After his departure, he went to Ephesus. During his three-year stay there, he heard reports of wickedness and division within the Corinthian church. In an effort to correct these evils, Paul wrote several letters to them, including the Epistle of First Corinthians.

1:1–9	The introductory remarks of Paul.
1:10–16	Paul condemns the divisions in the church and exhorts its members to unity.
1:17—2:16	Paul defends his ministry. He has preached the wisdom of Christ crucified. This wisdom is foolishness to the world, but is the glory of all those to whom the Spirit of God has revealed the truthfulness of it.
3:1–5	Paul declares that the simplicity of his teaching was due to the carnal state of the Corinthians, which state is clearly evidenced by their divisions.
3:6–23	Jesus Christ is the only foundation. Ministers are mere servants; the work is God's.
4:1–6	The duty of ministers is faithfulness.
4:6–21	Paul contrasts the arrogance and conceit of the false teachers to the humility and sacrifice of the apostles. Using his unique position as their spiritual father, Paul calls on the Corinthian believers to be discerning.
5:1–13	Flagrant, sexual immorality was being practiced by one of the members of the congregation. Paul reproves

	their lack of discipline and calls for expulsion of the guilty party.
6:1–11	Christians should not bring their legal disputes before heathen judges.
6:12–20	Paul reprimands the perversion of the principle of Christian liberty to excuse fornication. Our bodies belong to the Lord and should be devoted to His glory.
7:1–17	Paul answers their questions about marriage.
7:18–24	Paul advises that, provided they are not immoral or unlawful, our social positions should remain intact after coming to Christ.
7:25–40	Paul answers their questions about virgins and widows.
8:1–13	Christian liberty and conscience: was it lawful to eat meat that had been sacrificed to false gods?
9:1–23	Paul declares the right of ministers to be faithfully supported by their congregation.
9:24—10:13	Exhortations to self-denial.
10:14—11:1	While the purchase of meat offered to idols is a matter of conscience, attendance at the heathen feasts of sacrifice is idolatry, even if such was not their intention.
11:2–16	Men and women should take care to conform to the customs of dress in their community that assure modesty and properly reflect the man to be "the glory of God" and the woman to be "the glory of the man."
11:17–34	Paul exhorts the Corinthians to properly partake of the Lord's Supper.
12:1–31	Paul answers their questions about spiritual gifts. He reminds them that they are all members of one body. God has distributed these gifts so that each member may perform the function it is designed for.

13:1–13	Love [*agápe* {26}] is superior to all other gifts.
14:1–25	The gift of prophecy is more valuable than the gift of tongues.
14:26–40	Principles for orderly public worship.
15:1–34	Paul proves the fact of the resurrection of Christ. It is the foundation of our faith and the surety of our own resurrection.
15:35–58	Paul explains the nature of our resurrection.
16:1–9	Paul's specific instructions for the collection of monies from several Greek congregations for the poverty-stricken saints in Palestine.
16:10–12	Recommendations for Timothy and Apollos to be accepted by the Corinthians.
16:13–24	Paul's final admonition to them to stand firm in the faith. Salutation.

1 Cor. 16:1 | *Corinthian Christians Give to Jerusalem Saints*

Now concerning the collection for the saints, as indeed I arranged among the churches of Galatia, you also do likewise.

There were certain problems in the Corinthian church which were of great concern. Corinth was one of the most problematic churches of the apostolic age and was the cause of much heaviness of heart to the Apostle Paul. In fact, we would be appalled today to find some things tolerated in our churches which were tolerated in Corinth—drunkenness and gluttony at church gatherings while others stood by hungry, shocking immorality, participation in idolatrous feasts, and many other such sins which are found in the epistles to the Corinthians.

Paul does not disregard these matters, but he elaborates on them. We are glad because concerns of the Corinthians then are the same matters that concern us at the end of the Twentieth Century as we face a sinful and troublesome world. We need all the help and wisdom we can find to make it safely through these difficult times in which we live. Where could we find better advice and guidance than in the Word of God? "Your word *is* a lamp unto my feet, and a light unto my path" (Ps. 119:105).

"Now Concerning"

We are introduced to some of these matters by the Apostle Paul, the author of this epistle to the Corinthians, by the Greek preposition *perí* (4012), concerning. This refers to specific questions regarding matters that concerned them in view of certain circumstances which they were facing.

Other encounters with the word *perí* are found in 1 Corinthians 1:4, 14. There Paul takes the opportunity to deal with the important subject of marriage as it pertains to Christians. This chapter is a masterful discussion on the subject as related to the teaching of the Word of God (Matt. 5:27–32; 19:3–12; Mark 10:1–12; Luke 15:18).

Since Paul was a bachelor by choice, he could have excused himself by claiming that he was not qualified to speak on the subject. On the contrary, he accepted his duty as an apostle (1 Cor. 9:1) to make clear the Word of God (1 Thess. 4:15) on any subject that pertained to life in spite of his own choice concerning it. Thus we find Paul touching upon the subject of celibacy and marriage in 1 Corinthians 7:25–40. In this passage, the word *perí*, concerning, introduces the subject of celibacy and valid reasons for a celibate life.

The third subject that concerned the Corinthians was meats sacrificed to idols and the circumstances under which the Christian may or may not eat them. Paul again began with *perí* in his extended discussion of this subject in chapters 8, 9 and 10.

The fourth area of concern is spiritual gifts which Paul recognizes as existing among Christians. The subject is introduced in 1 Corinthians 12:1 again with the word *perí*. The discussion regarding spiritual gifts occupied the Apostle Paul greatly, for spiritual gifts affect the whole church as well as public worship. Therefore, he devotes chapters 12 to 14 to this subject.

Although Paul does not begin chapter 15 with the preposition *perí*, he takes the initiative on his own to let the Corinthians know the importance of the resurrection of the Lord Jesus Christ and that it is the basis of the Christian faith. Therefore, 1 Corinthians 15 is not merely an answer to a question of concern, but it is a matter of absolute theological necessity. This is why Paul begins chapter 15 with, "I make known [*gnōrízō* {1107}] to you." This word *gnōrízō* in this context certainly does not indicate speculative knowledge. It refers to divine knowledge which has become his own experience and has been the experience of every Christian. It is related to *gnṓsis* (1108), a word sometimes used to express knowledge which comes from God and is experienced by man.

Thus, after Paul discusses the resurrection of Christ and believers, he comes back to the daily functions of life. He asserts that no believer lives unto himself and dies unto himself (Rom. 14:7). Believers are the body of Christ (Eph. 5:30) who recognize other Christians who are in the body of Christ also, and who have the responsibility to help one another as they try to bring a Christian influence on the world in which they all live.

Therefore, the subject which Paul undertakes now constitutes still another concern, and we find 1 Corinthians 16 also beginning with the word *perí*, concerning: "Concerning the collection." Paul assumes that one body of Christians could not be indifferent to the needs of another body of Christians. They should be concerned.

"The Collection"

The first Christian church which was established at Jerusalem when the Holy Spirit came upon the assembled disciples (Acts 2:4) was a growing church. As a result of Peter's preaching, three thousand souls were saved and added to the church at Jerusalem in one day (Acts 2:41)! With large numbers came not only opportunities, but also problems. The church had the opportunity of teaching, of fellowship, and of breaking bread and praying together (Acts 2:42). With the first sermon by Peter in Jerusalem the words of Christ in John 14:12 were fulfilled: "Verily, verily I say unto you, he that believeth on Me, the works that I do shall he do also; and greater *works* than these shall he do; because I go unto My Father." Imagine, three thousand souls added to the church at one time!

The first thing that took place among believers was a concern by those who had material goods for those who did not, and there must have been many of them, for the first official appointment of service was to minister to the widows. The very word "widows" was synonymous with need (Acts 6:1–6). It is interesting, indeed, that the word "fellowship" in Greek is *koinōnía* (2842) (Acts 2:42). The word *koinōnía*, however, derives from *koiná*, the plural form of *koinós* (2839), common, which occurs in Acts 2:44 where we find that those who believed had everything in common. Therefore, "fellowship" is to have everything in common with our fellow believers. And then in verse 45 we see that among the believers were some who had material possessions; however, the moment they became believers, they considered those possessions as belonging not only to themselves, but to those of their brethren who had need: "And sold their possessions and goods, and parted them to all *men*, as every man had need." Faith produced compassion and voluntary sharing with those who had less. Indeed, this is as the Lord had ordained it in Matthew 6:1–4. It was inconceivable to the Lord how anyone could be called a believer who was not willing to help those in need. One who is not willing to sell what he has so that others may obtain what they need is not worthy of the kingdom of God. The Lord Jesus said in Mark 10:21, "One thing you lack: go your way, sell whatever you have, and give to the poor, and you shall have treasure in heaven; and come, take up the cross, and follow Me." When the work of grace is done in a person's heart, that heart is made willing to do that which Christ ordained, and only He enables a man to do what he would not be willing to do otherwise. "Sell what you have, and give alms; provide yourselves bags which wax not old, a treasure in heaven that fails not, where no thief approaches, neither moths corrupt" (Luke 12:33).

The poverty and need that existed within the Jerusalem church became known to the other churches that were established outside of Palestine as a result of Paul's endeavors. One such church was established in Rome. Paul writes to them in Romans 12:13: "Distributing to the necessity of saints; given to hospitality." He had also established the church in Ephesus to which he wrote in Ephesians 4:28: "Let him that stole steal no more: but rather let him labor, working with *his* hands the thing which is good, that he may have to give to him that needs."

And for individual Christians, Paul advises in 1 Timothy 6:18, "That they do good, that they be rich in good works, ready to distribute, willing to communicate." This word "communicate" also comes from *koinōnikoús*, the accusative plural masculine adjectival form of *koinōnikós* (2843), willing to consider what one has as common property (*koinós*). Here Paul declares the opportunity of the Corinthian church to show its concern for the Jerusalem church which was needy. Paul discreetly implies condemnation, and in this chapter he wants to tell them how they can learn generosity.

Paul took the initiative in helping the poor among the saints of Jerusalem: "Only *they would* that we should continue to remember [*mnēmoneúōmen*, the first person plural present active subjunctive form of *mnēmoneúō* {3421}, to remember] the poor; the same which I also was inclined to do" (Gal. 2:10). He was personally willing to go to Jerusalem to minister to the poor saints, for he said in Romans 15:25, 26, "But now I go unto

Jerusalem to minister unto the saints. For it has pleased them of Macedonia and Achaia to make a certain contribution for the poor saints which are in Jerusalem." And the Corinthians, who were in the process of collecting money for those needy saints in Jerusalem, were told by Paul: "Now concerning the collection for the saints. . . ." The word for "collection" here is a word that occurs in the New Testament only in 1 Corinthians 16:1, 2. It is *logía* (3048) from *lógos* (3056), word, or that which is selected, or *légō* (3004), to speak, to select. Its meaning is to collect appropriately. The collection of words makes communication possible and the collection of goods or money makes generosity possible. This means that they were not only to say they would do it, but to gather together or collect material means. Paul wanted their concern to be expressed in action and not mere words. In this context, the verb *légō*, to speak, originally meant "collect" as in the compound verb *sullégō* (4816), to gather. It is to gather little by little that which by itself may seem insignificant, but when put together with the other collections acquires significance. Even as words and sounds by themselves may mean nothing, when they are joined together with others, they become expressive of thought. This is exactly what the Apostle means here by the use of the word *logía*, collection. Your giving and my giving by themselves may seem very little, but together they become a lot.

Paul definitely gives the purpose for which material gifts were given as being "for the saints." "For" is the Greek *eis* (1519), for, to, and it shows the destination and the purpose for which the gifts of the Corinthian Christians were given. Although news traveled with difficulty at that time, the Corinthians had been informed somehow of the needs of the saints in Jerusalem. They did not ignore their need because these saints lived so far away, as Jerusalem is a great distance from Corinth. Furthermore, quite a number of the Corinthians were Gentile believers while the Jerusalem saints were Jewish believers. Neither the distance nor the nationality made any difference (Gal. 3:28). The Corinthians did not differentiate between home and foreign mission offerings. From this we can learn that we are not to ignore our needy brothers and sisters in Christ whom we cannot see and will probably never know. It does not matter that they may be on the other side of the world; it is still our responsibility to be concerned for them and to pray for and help them to the utmost. These believers in Corinth practiced what Hebrews 13:16 commands, "But to do good. . . ." "Good" comes from the Greek *eupoiía* (2140), to do benevolence or beneficence, which stands for good accomplishment, not only good speech in its initiation, but in its result. This stands in contrast to *euergesía* (2108), good work. Verse 16 continues: "And to communicate [*koinōnías*, the genitive singular feminine of the noun *koinōnia*, fellowship, having everything in common] forget not: for with such sacrifices God is well pleased." This verse teaches us that the believer, as he gives alms, should not be concerned only with the giving, but also with the accomplishment of the purpose for which it is given. This principle of love in providing the needs of others ought to be manifested by every believer as expressed by the disciple of love, John, in 1 John 3:17: "But whoso has it good in this world, and sees his brother have need, and shuts up his bowels of compassion from him, how dwells the love of God in him?" To say one loves God is hypocrisy if it is not tangibly expressed to one's brother who has need. John emphasizes this in 1 John 4:20: "If a man say I love God, and hates his brother, he is a liar: for he who loves not his brother whom he has seen, how can he love God whom he has not seen?"

"For the Saints"

Paul is concerned that the saints be helped. Romans 15:26 tells us that these were poor (*ptōchoi* [4434], helpless paupers) saints in Jerusalem. It is the duty of Christians to help all who need it, but especially those who are of the household of faith (Gal. 6:10).

That these believers were extremely poor contradicts the "prosperity gospel" which some preach, claiming that Christianity is a doorway to health and wealth. This teaching is a total misunderstanding of 3 John 2. The poor, being helpless, recognize that if they are going to be helped, it must be by someone outside of themselves. That is, of course, Jesus Christ, and that is why so many of the poor gladly accept His help and are saved. James is justified when he says in James 2:5, 6, "Has not God chosen the poor of this world, rich in faith and heirs of the kingdom which He has promised to them who love Him? But you have dishonored the poor. Do not rich men oppress you, and drag you before the judgment seats?" Saints who look upon their needy fellow believers with disdain ought to hear the words of the Lord in Luke 6:20, 24, "Blessed are you poor: for yours is the kingdom of God." "Woe unto you that are rich! for you have received your consolation." Physical poverty as characterized by the Jerusalem saints did not inhibit Paul from calling them what they really were — "saints."

A saint (*hágios* [40]) here and throughout the New Testament means a believer in Jesus Christ (Eph. 1:1; Col. 1:2) or a Christian. Saints are not the ones who are declared to be saints by some churches, but they are called to be saints because of their faith in Jesus Christ and their exemplary character (Rom. 1:7). It is interesting, indeed, that in Scripture the word "saint" is never applied to individuals as such. The Word of God does not speak of Saint Paul and Saint John, for instance. The word is always in the plural, saints (*hágioi*). As applied to individuals, it is used in the singular in 1 Corinthians 7:34 in an adjectival form; in Phillipians 4:21, Paul writes, "Salute every saint in Christ Jesus. The brethren which are with me greet you" and in Revelation 22:11, we read, "He that is unjust, let him be unjust still: and he who is filthy, let him be filthy still: and he that is righteous, let him be righteous still: and he that is holy [*hágios*], let him be holy still." Only Jesus in the New Testament is called "the Holy One" (Mark 1:24).

"As Indeed I Arranged"

Paul took the lead in initiating and organizing the collection for the poor saints in Jerusalem. This is indicated by the word *hṓsper* (5618) which is derived from *hōs* (5613), as, and the emphatic enclitic particle *per* (4007), indeed, wholly, exactly like. No minister of the gospel ought to be apathetic and inactive in view of fellow believers who are in need. There is nothing wrong with asking believers to help their needy brothers and sisters in Christ.

In a speech that Paul gave to the Ephesian elders who visited him at Miletus, he said in Acts 20:35, "I have shown you all things, how that so laboring you ought to support the weak, and to remember the words of the Lord Jesus, how He said, 'It is more blessed to give than to receive.' " One of the most important, yet most neglected, gifts of the spirit is mentioned in 1 Corinthians 12:28. In English it is called "helps." This is translated from the Greek *antilḗmpseis*, the plural of *antilḗmpsis* or *antílēpsis* (484), derived from the verb *antilabánō* (482) or in the middle voice *antilabánomai,* meaning to help or relieve. The verb actually refers to taking firm hold of someone in order to help him or her.

What the Gift of "Helps" Should Accomplish

Whereas the gift of "helps" is a sadly neglected gift, it is most needful. It is not only beneficial for the receiver, but also for the giver. It is an immeasurable blessing to the Christian to help others and an answer to the prayers of the needy. The gift of helps implies the gifts of healings, the workings of miracles, prophecy, discernments of the spirits, the families of languages, the interpretation of those languages (1 Cor. 12:9, 10) and administrations (1 Cor. 12:28). *Charísmata* (5486) are the results of grace (*cháris* [5485]), and if these gifts were to be epitomized in one word, that word would be "helps." You can help someone by healing him, by speaking the message that he needs either to admonish him or to comfort him, by understanding his spirit and discerning his exact need, by speaking to him in his own language, and if unable to make yourself understood, to have what you are telling him interpreted by another in order to teach him. These are all gifts which are helping people. Helping the saints of Jerusalem involved providing for the needs which they had, needs of the body or needs of their spiritual makeup. However, it is quite probable that sending money to the needy saints of Jerusalem was the only way the Corinthian believers could minister to them in their particular need.

Other Words Used Expressing the Gift of "Helps"

Besides the word *logía*, collection of money, which is intimated here in 1 Corinthians 16:1, Paul uses several words throughout his epistles to indicate the possible accomplishment of these collections.

We find three words all used in 2 Corinthians 8:4: "Praying us [the Macedonian Christians] with much entreaty that we would receive the gift [*chárin* {5484}, favor, the accusative of *cháris*, grace], and *take upon us* the fellowship [*koinōnía*, fellowship, partnership] of the ministering [*diakonía* {1248}, ministry] to the saints." Paul is speaking here of the gift which the Macedonian believers were sending to the needy Jerusalem believers, thus practicing the gift of helps which the Holy Spirit gave them.

The first of these gifts was *cháris*, the communication of the grace of God through the believers of Macedonia. They were favors to them. The main underlying characteristic of *cháris* is that it is an undeserved favor which causes change in the recipient. The first question that a helper should ask is not whether the one being helped deserves it, but whether he needs it and whether the help is going to effect a change in his character and circumstance.

The second gift was *koinōnía*, fellowship, sharing what one has with another who has need or has less than the one helping. As we explained earlier in this chapter, the noun *koinōnía* derives from the adjective *koinós*, common, to be shared. A believer should consider his possessions as common property if needed by others. This was the philosophy of the early Christians (Acts 2:44; 4:32). In 2 Corinthians 9:13 where the word *koinōnía* occurs with the same meaning, it is said that it is to be practiced in liberality (*haplótēs* [572], openhandedness). In Romans 15:26, we find the believers in Macedonia and Achaia helping the Jerusalem saints, and, again, it is called *koinōnía,* only here it is distinguished as being offered to the poor (*ptōchoí*, helpless, indicating abject poverty).

The third word found in 2 Corinthians 8:4, as a loose synonym of the gift of helps or collection, is the word *diakonía*, service, ministry. The word implies relief or alms, contributions (Acts 11:29; Rom. 15:31; 2 Cor. 8:4; 9:1, 13; 11:8; Rev. 2:19). It speaks of a distribution or administration of alms collected (Acts 6:1; 12:25; 2 Cor. 9:12). *Diakonía* involves compassionate love towards the needy within the Christian community (Acts 6:1, 4; 2 Cor. 8:4; 9:12, 13; Rev. 2:19). It is the grace that meets the needs of others, whatever those needs are. In order that this ministry may be made possible and done properly, it is necessary for the discernment of needs to be exercised. The ministry that the Corinthians could render to the poor saints of Jerusalem was so obvious that it needed no reminder or expounding by Paul (2 Cor. 9:1). Their ministry provided a test of this obedience and generosity of what should be considered as common property (v. 13).

Another synonym of the gift of helps is what Paul calls *hadrótēs* (100), bounty. From what we read in 2 Corinthians 8:16–20, we come to the conclusion that this help sent to the poor saints of the Jerusalem church was so significant that it was considered a bounty. In fact, it was so large that it was taken to them not only by Titus, but by someone else who was assigned to accompany him. They did not give the responsibility to only one person to transport it. It is challenging to us to note that this gift, which was so large, was given out of the deep poverty and affliction of the Macedonians. In fact, they gave above and beyond their ability, even begging Paul to receive their contribution for the ministering to the saints (2 Cor. 8:1–5). I wonder how many of us would show such generosity to our needy fellow Christians. The basis of the Macedonian's giving as noted in verse 5 was that they "first gave their own selves to the Lord, and unto us by the will of God." If we are to give generously, it must proceed from this basis also.

In 2 Corinthians 9:5, Paul calls this gift *eulogía* (2129), blessing. The word derives from *eu* (2095), good, and *lógos*, the noun from the verb *légō*, to speak, which it has come to mean, although originally it meant to gather. "To speak" is to gather words and fit them together. The word *logía* or *logeía* which is found in 1 Corinthians 16:1, and translated "collection of money," may very well have come from *légō* which had the meaning "to collect." Therefore, the noun *eulogía* may stand for a collection that is for a good purpose, which was the case of the gift sent by the churches of Macedonia and others for the poor saints of Jerusalem. In this verse, the gift for the Jerusalem church is twice called *eulogía*, blessing, or a benevolent collection. It was a double blessing, for it blessed the giver and the receiver alike.

In 2 Corinthians 9:12, the help sent is called *leitourgía* (3009), public service or public collection. This indicates to us that the need was publicly known and the collection was also public.

There are two more words which were used by the Apostle Paul when giving his defense before Felix in Acts 24:17. One is "alms" (*eleēmosúnē* [1654]). The word comes from *éleos* (1656), mercy, which is the expression of compassion or pity toward someone in need in contrast to *cháris*, grace, which refers to grace and kindness, without reference to the need of the individual. The second word is *prosphorá* (4376), offering, derived from the preposition *prós* (4314), toward, and the verb *phérō* (5342), to bring. It means that which we bring to God as an offering.

Therefore, the gifts of money collected from many and sent to the Jerusalem church were voluntarily given because they were needed, not deserved. They were given because the Christians knew that their possessions should be in common with other Christians.

"Among the Churches of Galatia, You Also Do Likewise"

Paul is writing to the corporate body of the church in Corinth (1 Cor. 1:2). His instructions about the collection for the saints in Jerusalem had apparently been given to the churches of Galatia also, probably on his departure from Corinth, sailing from the port of Cenchreae on the Saronic Gulf, approximately seven miles from Corinth.

Which were the churches of Galatia? They were Antioch, Pisidia, Iconium, Lystra, and Derbe. These were churches established by the Apostle Paul on his first missionary journey.

Timothy was a native of either Derbe or Lystra where the Apostle Paul first enlisted help for the saints of Jerusalem. He now urges the Corinthian church to do what the Galatian churches had done.

LESSONS:

1. It is right for Christian leaders to enlist the help of one church for another.
2. To take a collection for needy saints in another place is a Christian duty.
3. The Galatian churches of Antioch, Pisidia, Iconium, Lystra, and Derbe were churches in Galatia which the Apostle Paul enlisted to help the saints of Jerusalem.
4. He admonishes the Corinthian church to do as the churches of Galatia had done.
5. Both the giver and the receiver are blessed when the one who has shares with the one who has not.

1 Cor. 16:2 | How the Collections Were to Be Made

On every first day of the week, let each one of you by himself put aside a certain sum of money according to the way he has been prospered, so that when I come no collections will have to be made.

In the previous verse, the Apostle Paul had urged the Corinthian Christians to share their blessings with needy Christians in other areas. He now proceeds to detail the way it should be done.

"On the First Day of Every Week"

Here the Apostle Paul recognizes which day the Corinthians gathered together for worship. It was on the day after the Sabbath day, an important day that was to be distinguished from other days. The exact phrase with which this verse begins is *katá* (2596), a distributive preposition meaning "on each"; *mían*, the accusative singular feminine numeral of *héís* (1520), one; *Sabbátōn*, the genitive plural of the noun *Sábbaton* (4521), Sabbath. Thus we have the first day after every Sabbath designated as the Day of the Lord, or what is today known as Sunday (Rev. 1:10). This was the day of Christian worship in celebration of the Lord's resurrection which occurred on Sunday. Such is the day expressed in Matthew 28:1; Mark 16:2, 9; Luke 24:1; John 20:1,

19, and Acts 20:7. In Luke 18:12 and Mark 16:9 *Sábbaton*, Sabbath in the singular, means week. The first day of the week is never called "Sabbath" in the Scriptures. The Lord Jesus taught that it was proper to use the Sabbath day to show benevolence (Matt. 12:12; Mark 3:4). Paul has instructed the Galatian churches and now the Corinthian church to collect money for benevolent purposes on the first day of the week.

"Let Each One of You"

"Each one of you" is translated from the Greek *hékastos* (1538), each one; *humṓn*, the genitive plural of the second person personal pronoun *sú* (4771), of you. This indicates that giving for benevolent purposes was a private matter decided upon by each individual. The sum of money to be given was not stipulated by the Apostle Paul. No minimum and no maximum is designated. This is left to the individual conscience, for Christianity does not consist of rules and regulations, but of a relationship with God.

In the Old Testament, the Lord wanted the Israelites to realize that all things come from God and that His partnership ought not to be forgotten, but tangibly remembered by the minimum of a tithe (Lev. 27:30–33; Num. 18:21–32). The Lord, however, in Matthew 23:23, castigated the Jews for giving their tithe without thought as to what it signified. "Woe unto you, scribes and Pharisees, hypocrites! for you pay tithe of mint and anise and cumin, and have omitted the weightier *matters* of the law, judgment, mercy, and faith: these you ought to have done, and not to leave the other undone."

But if, without faith, we do anything out of mere custom or obedience to the law, it is of no value. If we perform an action apart from faith, then that action is worth very little to the one exercising it. The Lord emphasized that whatever we do should be the result of faith. Faith is born of repentance (Luke 3:8ff.). When we repent of our sins and believe in Jesus Christ, He becomes the fulfillment of the law in our hearts (Matt. 5:17). We no longer need to be told what to do. Christ becomes our conscience (*suneídēsis* [4893] derived from *sún* [4862], conjointly together, and *eídō* [1492], to perceive, know). Upon receiving Christ as our indwelling Lord and Savior, we know together with Him what is our duty. God tells us, however, that in the measure in which we empty ourselves, He will fill us. Paul confirms this in Romans 12:3: "God has dealt to each man [*hekástō*, the dative singular masculine adjectival form of *hékastos,* to each one] individually." God does not pour out an equal amount of faith upon all, but He fills only the room that we leave for Him. The same thought is expressed in 1 Corinthians 3:5 where Paul says, "Even as the Lord gave to each man." Note that this is to **each** man (*hekástō*) and not to **every** man, pointing out the individuality of God's giving.

The Lord has made us all share in the common characteristics of humanity, but nevertheless, He deals with each one of us as individuals, filling the areas that we have surrendered to Him. "Everyone" or "whoever" would be expressed by the Greek word *pás* (3956), meaning any and every. In 1 Corinthians 7:7 Paul says, in recognition of the individual gifts that God gives, "But each man [*hékastos*] has his proper gift of God, one after this manner and another after that." To further elucidate the "each one," he adds the word *ídion* which in the King James Version is translated "his proper." To be more specific, it means "one's very own" or "private." The gifts of God are not poured out like the rain or sunshine upon all men, but are apportioned differently to each individual.

In 1 Corinthians 7:17, Paul says, "But as God has distributed to each man [*hekástō*], as the Lord has called each one [*hékaston*], so let him walk, and so ordain I in all churches." It is most significant that the verb that the Apostle Paul uses here and which is translated "ordain" is *diatássomai* (1299). This is the same verb that he uses in the aorist tense (*diétaxa*) in 1 Corinthians 16:1 which we translated "arranged." But Paul is not saying that he ordained or arranged the percentage or the exact sum that each individual should give, but that he arranged that this should be the process in all the churches of Galatia and now of Corinth.

The sum which each individual should give to the poor or for the relief of others is entirely in response to the work of Christ in one's heart. The standard is set in 2 Corinthians 9:7: "Each person [*hékastos*] according as he purposes in his heart, so let him give; not grudgingly, or of necessity: for God loves a cheerful giver." Oh, that every one of us could give the testimony which the Apostle Paul gave before the Sanhedrin in Acts 23:1: "And Paul, earnestly beholding the counsel, said, 'Men and brethren, I have lived in all good [*agathḗ*, the dative singular feminine adjectival form of *agathós* {18}, benevolent] conscience before God until this day.' " This was Paul's goal for the individuals in Corinth. He wanted each one to examine his conscience and give accordingly, and not that each one should give a stated sum of money.

"By Himself Put Aside a Certain Sum of Money"

Let him "put aside a certain sum of money." In the Greek, the expression is *par,* which stands for the preposition *pará* (3844), beside him, denoting close proximity; *heautṓ*, the dative singular masculine third person of the reflexive pronoun *heautoú* (1438), to himself; *tithétō*, the third person singular present active imperative of *títhēmi* (5087), to put, lay. This means that at the beginning of every week on the Lord's day, each believer in Corinth should himself lay aside a certain sum of money which would accumulate. This is expressed by the word *thēsaurízōn*, the nominative singular masculine present active participle of *thēsaurízō* (2343), to treasure up. The noun *thēsaurós* (2344) and the verb both derive from the verb *títhēmi*, to lay. Something laid aside little by little becomes a *thēsaurós*, a treasure.

Whereas the small amount that the poor man has stored up each week may not seem much to the rich man, yet it is his treasure to offer to God, and God accepts it as such. Remember Jesus Christ acknowledged the widow's mite (Mark 12:41–44), and of the woman who poured her box of ointment upon the Lord's head, He said, "She has done what she could" (Mark 14:8). Whereas the Lord taught us, "Lay not up for yourselves treasures upon earth where moth and rust does corrupt, and where thieves break through and steal" (Matt. 6:19), He nevertheless did say, "But lay up for yourselves treasures in heaven, where neither moth nor rust does corrupt, and where thieves do not break through nor steal" (v. 20). The treasuring up which the Apostle Paul suggests is not for selfish purposes, but for helping others. In actuality, this is treasuring up in heaven. Have you ever experienced the joy and excitement of saving up enough money, perhaps bit by bit, to meet some particular need on the mission field? What a sense of satisfaction this brings! This is "hilarious" giving (2 Cor. 9:7). The Lord gave us the parable of the rich farmer in Luke 12:13–21 to teach us that storing treasure for self is self-destructive for it leads to confidence being placed on earthly goods and not on God who, through His natural benevolence, makes this treasure possible.

"According to the Way He Has Been Prospered"

Earnings are not uniform. This is why Paul says one should lay aside a certain sum of money according to the measure in which he has been prospered. The Greek says *hó ti* (*ho*, the nominative singular neuter form of *hós* [3739] meaning "that which" and *ti*, the accusative singular neuter of the indefinite pronoun *tis* [5100], whatever), together meaning "that which" or "whatever that amount is." Loosely, it could be translated "according to the money that he has been able to earn during the week." *Án* (302) is an abbreviation of the suppositional conjunction of reality *eán* (1437). Together these words, *hó ti án*, mean that a person should lay aside that amount of money no matter how large or small it is.

The verb that follows is *euodṓtai* (MT), the third person singular present passive subjunctive of *euodóō* (2137) which is derived from *eu* (2095), good or well, and *hodós* (3598), a way, journey. It means "as his way should prosper." As his way prospers, he should give accordingly. This is an acknowledgment of the fact that the income of each one is not uniform, but varying.

The verb *euodoúmai*, the passive of *euodóō*, is used only three times in the New Testament. Paul, in Romans 1:10, writes, "Making request, if by any means now at length I might have a prosperous journey [*euodōthḗsomai*, the first person singular future passive indicative of *euodóō*] by the will of God to come unto you." Paul wanted to reach Rome, but he knew that could only come about by the will of God. The second occurrence is in 1 Corinthians 16:2 where it implies that what one earns during the week is also by the will of God. And the third time the verb occurs is in 3 John 2 (see the author's book on the Epistles of John). Our first concern should be for the prosperity of our souls; the health and prosperity of our bodies should be left in the hands of God. In our verse, the teaching is that our giving for the sustenance of the poor should be in proportion to the blessing that we have received from God. We are blessed of God, and in turn we bless others by sharing His blessing which, in turn, becomes a blessing to us again. One reason the Apostle Paul wanted the Corinthians to lay aside weekly what they wanted to give to the Jerusalem saints was so that they would not spend it all on themselves.

While the Apostle Paul encourages the believers of Corinth to share their God-given provision with the saints in Jerusalem, he does not want them to neglect their own needs and the needs of their household. In writing to Timothy in 1 Timothy 5:8 he says, "But if any provide not for his own, and especially for those of his own house, he has denied the faith, and is worse than an infidel." We are reminded here of our Lord's condemnation of the scribes and Pharisees in Mark 7:10–13. To avoid providing for their parents' need, they would say that their money was "Corban," or dedicated to God, and so they could not use it. It is doubtful if they ever did give it to God's work. This was just an excuse not to part with their money.

In 2 Corinthians 8:2, where Paul compares the Macedonians' generosity with the possible reluctance to share by the Corinthians, he uses the noun *perisseía* (4050) which in the King James Version is translated "abundance" (cf. 10:15). However, it means superfluity, an overflowing, something above the ordinary, indicating a conscious effort to abound in giving (Rom. 5:17; James 1:21). The natural tendency, when the Lord pours such superfluity upon us, is to increase our standard of living so that we consume more of what we have on ourselves and have nothing left over for others. The verb *perisseúō* (4052), in the King James Version translated "to abound," should be "to make abound," and is found in 2 Corinthians 8:2, 7 [twice]; 9:8 [twice], 12.

There is a difference between the verb *perisseúō* and the synonym *pleonázō* (4121) which is also translated "to abound." The verb *pleonázō* is found in 2 Corinthians 8:15 constituting a quotation from Exodus 16:18 regarding the practice of the Israelites in the desert as they gathered the manna for their daily needs. The quotation is: "As it is written, he that had gathered much had nothing over" [*ouk* {3756}, the absolute negative; *epleónase*, the third person singular aorist active indicative of *pleonázō,* to have more than enough]. Its real meaning could be described as greediness—the more one has, the more one wants, and there is no surplus left for others in need. This is the word from which the noun *pleonexía* (4124), covetousness or greed, is derived. When God blesses and we gather more than enough, our appetite for more may grow, and we consider the abundant provision of God as not enough even for ourselves. On the other hand, the opposite verb is used in the second phrase of this quotation: "And he that had gathered little had no [*ouk*, the absolute negative] lack [*ēlatte āse*, the third person singular aorist active indicative of *elattonéō* {1641} from the adjective *élattōn* {1640}, less, found only here in the NT]."

From these two verbs then, we understand the meaning of *perisseúō* of 2 Corinthians 8:7. It is to have enough for oneself and surplus to share with others. The believer ought to learn and apply to himself the meaning of this important word in the Christian vocabulary. A genuine Christian does not consider only his needs and those of his family, but always has a heart of compassion and generosity for others. This is why Paul, in 2 Corinthians 8:2, says of the Macedonians that their "deep poverty abounded [*eperísseusen*] unto the riches of their liberality." You do not have to be rich to be generous; it is only necessary to restrict your demands for selfish purposes. Then God will bless and reward you for your generosity in serving others. This is what the Apostle Paul means by equality (*isótēs* [2471]), the definition of which is clearly stated in 2 Corinthians 8:14:

> But by an equality, *that* now at this time your abundance [*perísseuma* {4051}, that which is left over, whereas *perisseía* is the attitude of making something suffice for oneself and for others] *may be a supply* for their want [*hustérēma* {5303}, lack, deficiency], that their abundance [*perísseuma*] also may be *a supply* for your want; that there may be equality.

Equality, then, for the Apostle Paul was the voluntary sharing with others through *perisseía*; that is, no matter how much or how little one had, he would make it suffice for his own needs and also for the poor. Of course, the same also applies to opulence, that which is left over (*pleónasma* [n.f.]) from one's own abundance that he cannot use for himself. So the rich exercise generosity out of opulence while the poor from *perisseía*, a conscious effort of limiting one's own needs and thus consciously having a surplus for others! According to God's Word, all believers are to share whether they have much or little.

So the Apostle Paul, in writing to the Corinthians to put aside a sum of money each week for the poor saints of Jerusalem, did not appeal only for the surplus of the rich, but even to the conscious saving of the poor who always seem to have a generous spirit in spite of their poverty (*ptōcheía*). Thus, little by little, a treasure (*thēsaurós*) would accumulate for the poor saints of Jerusalem. What a joy for somebody who could not ordinarily give a large sum of money to be able to share his treasure which he had collected little by little.

"So That When I Come No Collections Will Have to Be Made"

What a joy for the Corinthian believers to know that each had done so much, and for the Apostle Paul to commend them by saying, You see how much you are able to give for the poor saints in Jerusalem!

These believers never would have been able to give as much had they taken an offering at the appearance of Paul, but each week, according to Paul's counsel, they laid aside a portion for the needy. God evidently had blessed them, and their income proved enough to meet their own needs and those of others. Thus, they could be counted as rich, not because they were able to satisfy any desire they may have had, but because they restricted their own desires so that the lack of others might be supplied. It was Socrates who wisely said that it is not the person who has much who is rich, but the one who has few desires.

The Golden Text concerning giving is found in 2 Corinthians 9:7 which, when correctly translated, says, "Each person according as he purposes [*proaireítai*, the third person singular present middle deponent indicative of *proairéomai* {4255}, purposes, resolves, derived from the preposition *pró* {4253}, before, in preference, and *airéō* {138}, to choose, that is, a predetermined choice] in his heart."

The next phrase shows the attitude which should be expressed in our giving:

> Not out of sorrow [*mḗ* {3361}, the relative 'not' showing that in our human weakness we sometimes do give grudgingly; *ek* {1537}, out of; *lúpēs*, the genitive singular feminine of the noun *lúpē* {3077}, sorrow, regret] or of necessity [*anágkēs*, the genitive singular feminine noun *anágkē* {318}, necessity, a requirement]: for God loves a cheerful [*hilarón*, the accusative singular masculine of the adjective *hilarós* {2431}, cheerful, joyful] giver.

This Greek word for "cheerful" is found only in this verse, although in Romans 12:8 we find the noun *hilarótēs* (2432), cheerfulness or gladness. This implies that giving is not something that one has to do, but something that the Christian joyfully chooses to do resulting from our condition as "partakers of the divine nature" (2 Pet. 1:4). He never regrets giving for it is the joy of his life, nor will he give grudgingly. Giving, for the Christian, is not mandated, and the measure of his personal joy is multiplied by his altruism.

Second Corinthians 9:8 should be understood in the context of verse 7:

> And God is able to make all grace [*chárin* {5484}, favor, whatever a Christian is able to do to relieve others] abound [*perisseúsai*, the aorist active infinitive of *perisseúō*, to be sufficient to meet one's own needs and also those of others] toward you; that you, always having all sufficiency [*autárkeian*, the accusative singular feminine of the noun *autárkeia* {841}, self-sufficiency] in all things, may abound [*perisseuēte*, the second person plural present active subjunctive of *perisseúō*] to every good [*agathón*, the accusative singular neuter of the adjective *agathós* {18}, benevolent] work.

The word *chárin* (favor) occurs in verse 3 as a synonym of *logía* (collection). We shall examine this in our next chapter. It indicates that, little by little, that which the Corinthians had been able to accumulate had become a collection of significance that would bestow great blessing on those who were suffering and needy. Therefore, let no believer look with disdain upon the little that he or she can put aside every week for the furtherance of God's work. God does not judge according to the size of the gift, but according to the attitude of the giver.

LESSONS:

1. The intimation of this verse is that the working week consisted of Monday through Friday. Saturday was a day of rest, and the first day after each Sabbath, now known as Sunday, should be our day of worship because of the resurrection of Jesus Christ.
2. On the Lord's day, we should reflect upon the goodness of God who has made provision for us as a result of our work.
3. Giving for the relief of others is entirely a voluntary act, and it should be gauged according to God's provision for us.
4. Each one should attempt to make what God has provided suffice for himself and his household needs, and in addition, the needs of others.
5. A little added each week accumulates to a treasure which becomes a privilege for each believer to give to the collection and will be rewarded accordingly.
6. That collection becomes a source of blessing for those who give it and for those to whom it is given.

1 Cor. 16:3 | *Those Entrusted with Money Must Be Honest*

And when I arrive, those whom you would approve through letters, them shall I send to transport your gracious gift to Jerusalem.

The offerings every week for the poor saints in Jerusalem continued for approximately one year (2 Cor. 8:10; 9:2). They were collections from the Gentile churches in Philippi, Thessalonica, Corinth, and Galatia to the mother Jewish church in Jerusalem. The gospel came to the Gentiles from the Jews in Jerusalem, and Paul recognizes this indebtedness in Romans 15:27: "It has pleased them verily; and their debtors they are. For if the Gentiles have been made partakers of their spiritual things, their duty is also to minister unto them in carnal things." The collections were in gratitude for the spiritual gifts of the Jerusalem church.

In Galatians 6:6 Paul says, "Let him that is taught in the Word communicate unto him that teaches in all good things." And in 1 Corinthians 9:11, he says, "If we have sown unto you spiritual things, is it a great thing if we shall reap your carnal things?" The Apostle Paul was conscious of his special calling to the Gentiles. His satisfaction was exceedingly great that his ministry among them was successful and so many churches had been established that they could now acknowledge their spiritual debt by material offerings to the Jews from whom the gospel came. This is why in Romans 15:16 he says, "That I should be the minister of Jesus Christ to the Gentiles, ministering the gospel of God, that the offering up of the Gentiles might be acceptable, being sanctified by the Holy Ghost."

"And When I Arrive"

Since Paul fully intended to go to Corinth, he said, "And when I arrive [*paragénōmai*, the first person singular second aorist middle deponent subjunctive of *paragínomai* {3854} which is derived from the preposition of proximity *pará* {3844}, to, at, and *gínomai* {1096}, to be, come, arrive]." Paul was looking forward to his visit to Corinth, and one of the first things he envisioned was sending help to the needy brethren in Jerusalem. However, he did not plan to take the collection to Jerusalem by himself, but instructed that others approved by the church of Corinth should go. Thus they would experience the joy of participating in supplying the needs of others.

"Those Whom You Would Approve Through Letters"

Paul speaks of "those whom you would approve [*dokimásēte*, the second person plural aorist active subjunctive of *dokimázō* {1381}, to test and approve] through letters." The approved delegates from Corinth had commendatory letters from the whole church. This was an accepted introduction of the delegates from one church to another (Acts 15:23–29; Rom. 16:1, 2; 2 Cor. 8:16–24). There was a limited number of these letters called "epistles" (*epistolḗ* [1992]) which had general instructive purposes. In English, we differentiate the limited letter by simply calling it a letter, and the general instructive document we refer to as an epistle. Paul wanted the Corinthians to designate by a letter or letters their approval of the people whom they were going to send to Jerusalem.

The Apostle Paul does not indicate the exact way whereby the carriers of the collection should be tested and approved, but that it was testing for this particular task is demonstrated by the aorist subjunctive form of the verb *dokimásēte*, to test, approve. The people selected were surely men of integrity, but Paul thought that they should be approved for the particular task of being entrusted with the large amount of money to be carried to Jerusalem.

"Them Shall I Send"

Paul was a wise man. He did not want to do the testing and approving himself, for he wanted to be above and beyond any possibility of criticism. It would certainly not look right to both choose and approve the carriers of this money; however, he did reserve the right to approve the decision of the congregation, and this is why he said, "Them will I send." Paul was still the leader in the Corinthian church. When an immoral act was revealed between a young man and his stepmother, Paul did not ignore it although he was away from the church (see 1 Cor. 5). He considered himself present in the spirit, and he instructed the congregation to act as if he were present. However, he wanted them to make the necessary decisions themselves. Paul was careful not to give the impression that he was dictatorial. In this case, he wanted the local congregation to appoint and to attest those to whom they were going to entrust transporting the collection to the saints of Jerusalem. He did not want, however, to neglect his proper responsibility which he willingly assumed after taking precautions against possible criticism.

"To Transport Your Gracious Gift to Jerusalem"

Observe that Paul says, "**You** test and approve" and "**I** will send them." He did not say, "**I** will transport," but "**Them** shall I send to transport your gracious gift." They and not Paul were to transport the gift, for that could possibly cause suspicion against himself, and humanly speaking, he wanted to eliminate that.

"To transport your gracious gift" is expressed through the second aorist active infinite *apenegkeín.* This is from the verb *apophérō* (667), to bring from, derived from the preposition *apó* (575), from, and *phérō* (5342), to carry. They were to be entrusted with the task of carrying the collection from those who gave it to those who were going to receive it in Jerusalem. People who are to be entrusted with money ought to give evidence that they are trustworthy.

The money which had been collected over a period of time and which they were given to take to Jerusalem was called *logía* (3048), collection, contribution (vv. 1, 2). However, in verse 3, this same collection is called *chárin* (5484), gracious gift, because it is the accusative of the word *cháris* (5485), grace which has the power to change a person or situation. In 2 Corinthians 8:4, it is also called *chárin* in demonstration that the gift of money, when given by believers for a certain specific purpose, can change a situation for the better. I believe this is why the collection of money is called *chárin,* for it has a benevolent effect on believers who are struggling with a situation far less favorable than normal circumstances. How wonderful, indeed, for believers to know that their money given for other believers can have such an encouraging effect! Although money, itself, cannot produce the effect desired by the giver, when it is given in the name of the Lord, it invokes the prayer of believers for the power of God to be enacted. God then grants His power, and both the givers and the recipients enjoy God's blessing.

<u>LESSONS</u>:

1. This verse begins with "And when I arrive." But the verb *paragénōmai* is the second aorist middle deponent subjunctive of *paragínomai* which

makes the human plan of Paul to return to Corinth subject to the divine will. Paul was totally dependent upon God making the circumstances possible, and thus making His will evident. Planning is always wise, but it should be subject to the divine will.

2. Paul wanted the Corinthians to be ready: first, they should have enough collected to make it worthwhile to send it to Jerusalem, and second, there should be those qualified and attested to carry it there.
3. Paul expresses the trust to be placed on the choice that the Corinthian church would make of those qualified to transport their gift, and he requested that they should be certified by letters to him. Testing and approving by the majority is the divine plan of action.
4. Paul, in spite of the fact that he is an apostle, shows willingness to accept their choice and attestation.
5. Paul calls the collection the "gracious giving" of the Corinthians because he fully expected the help provided to have a benevolent effect on the recipients.

1 Cor. 16:4 | Paul's Evaluation of a Situation

And if it be worthwhile for me to go also, they will go with me.

The Apostle Paul wanted the Corinthian collection for the needy believers in Jerusalem to be ready when he came to Corinth and the men who were going to transport it to be fully attested to by the church. However, up until this point, he was not sure whether he would go with the delegates to take the collection to the saints in Jerusalem. He wanted to evaluate the situation when the time came and then decide and act accordingly. He would not be obstinate regarding a decision made previously and impose it on the Corinthian church.

"And if It Be Worthwhile for Me to Go Also"

Paul begins this verse with "if" (*eán* [1437]) which is sometimes used in the sense of "when and if," but in this instance seems merely to indicate that Paul had not made up his mind.

"If it be [*ḗ*, the third person singular present subjunctive of *eimí* {1510}, to be]" indicates that the evaluation would be made of the situation when the proper time came. I can imagine the joy of Paul over the prospect of taking this collection personally to the church in Jerusalem. In Romans 15:17, 18 Paul says, "I have therefore whereof I may glory through Jesus Christ in those things which pertain to God. For I will not dare to speak anything which Christ has not wrought by me, to make Gentiles obedient, by word and deed." Paul wanted to leave the matter open so that he could make a proper evaluation of the situation, whether it was helpful or worthwhile (*áxion*, the accusative singular masculine adjectival form of *áxios* [514], worthwhile) for him to go along with the other delegates. Some of the delegates were from other churches listed in Acts 20:4. There were seven men, plus Luke, who came with Paul (v. 4) to bring offerings to Jerusalem. Their names are Sopater of Berea, Aristarchus and Secundus of Thessalonica, Gaius of Derbe, Timothy of Lystra, and Tychicus and Trophimus of Asia. These went ahead to Troas and waited there for Paul. It was there that Luke met them (Acts 20:5).

"They Will Go with Me"

In this last phrase, Paul asserts his apostolicity and the initiative that he had taken in the matter of this collection, especially among the Corinthians. Paul wanted the Jerusalem saints to know that he cared for them. Actually, the Jewish believers had a fear of Paul, not knowing whether he was a true disciple or not, for he had severely persecuted the church before his conversion (Acts 9:26–31). By going himself to deliver the contribution to the needy, although he was an apostle to the Gentiles, he showed his great love to them. Traveling certainly was not easy in those days, and the journey must have been arduous.

The preposition which Paul uses in this phrase is *sún* (4862), meaning conjointly with, and not *metá* (3326), meaning merely "with." They would go together as one unit. What a lovely thought that delegates from several different churches would join together as one to take relief to another church in need.

LESSONS:

1. Paul told the Corinthian church to designate people to take the collection to Jerusalem, but he was not sure whether it would be necessary for him to go also.
2. We learn from Acts 20 that Paul did go. He was eager to participate in sharing the blessings, and to assure the Christians in Jerusalem, whom he had persecuted prior to his conversion, of his love.
3. It is commendable when churches work together to help those in need.

1 Cor. 16:5 | *Paul's Plan to Return to Corinth*

I shall then come to you when I go through Macedonia, for I am now going through Macedonia.

Paul had preached the gospel at Philippi, Thessalonica, and Berea, before moving into the region of Achaia of which Corinth was the principal city (Acts 16:9). Paul preached the gospel in Athens, which was part of Achaia, and then came to Corinth where he had ministered eighteen months (Acts 18:1–17). At that time, Paul had crossed the narrow piece of land from Corinth to Cenchrea, and from there he set sail for Ephesus. He had labored in Ephesus for two years, and from there he wrote this first letter to the Corinthians (Acts 19:1–41).

"I Shall Then Come to You When I Go through Macedonia"

Paul was planning to come back to Corinth through Macedonia, the northernmost province of Greece. It was Paul's ardent desire to take the collections from the Corinthians to the saints in Jerusalem and to personally share in the delivery of their gracious gift. The work in Corinth had not been easy, but God blessed Paul's perseverance; a church had been established there, and he longed to see the Corinthian believers again. "I shall then come to you," he wrote. The Greek verb used is *eleúsomai*, first person singular future middle deponent indicative of *érchomai*

(2064), to come. That was the expression of his human desire and plan. He had not seen the Corinthians in the two years in which he ministered in Ephesus.

Paul was not ignorant of the distressing situation which existed among the Corinthians, but he was glad for the collection for the needy saints in Jerusalem in which they had participated. In spite of the fact that the Corinthian church was the most wealthy, it was the least promising. It seems that the hope of Paul for a most generous offering from the Corinthian church was somewhat disappointing, for it was not even mentioned in Acts 20:4, although the contributions of other churches were. In 2 Corinthians 8 and 9, Paul discusses the disproportionate Corinthian contribution, considering their ability to give, and the sacrificial Macedonian contribution.

Paul tells the Corinthians of his plan to visit the Macedonian churches on his way to Corinth, namely the churches of Philippi, Thessalonica, and Berea. He wanted to see what the results of his preaching among them had been. It is not certain how many times Paul visited Corinth, but when he came the second time (2 Cor. 13:2) and the third time (2 Cor. 2:1; 12:14), he did not find the Corinthians the most spiritual people, but the most contentious. Consequently, he deemed that his attitude ought to be confrontational if it were going to be realistic. Thus, in 2 Corinthians 12:19–21, with deep sorrow, he evaluated the situation among the Corinthians:

> Again do you think that we excuse ourselves unto you? We speak before God in Christ: but we do all things, dearly beloved, for your edifying. For I fear, lest, when I come, I shall not find you such as I would, and that I shall be found unto you such as you would not: lest there be debates, envyings, wraths, strifes, backbitings, whisperings, swellings, tumults: and lest, when I come again, my God will humble me among you, and that I shall bewail many which have sinned already, and have not repented of the uncleanness and fornication and lasciviousness which they have committed.

Nevertheless, Paul says, "I shall come unto you."

"For I Am Now Going through Macedonia"

Paul wanted to retrace his steps in order to visit the churches of Macedonia and see how they were faring in their Christian behavior. In Philippians 4:1, Paul calls them his "joy and crown." In 1 Thessalonians 2:20, Paul calls them his "glory and joy." In speaking of the Bereans in Acts 17:11, he calls them "more noble" than the Thessalonians. No wonder, then, that Paul was eager to return to Corinth to see whether there was any spiritual growth among them. However, he must have been quite disappointed, for he found what he detailed in 2 Corinthians 12:19–21 a depressing situation, indeed.

LESSONS:

1. The Corinthian church that was founded by Paul was not one that was his glory and gave him the greatest amount of joy.
2. The trouble was not the ineffectiveness of the gospel that Paul preached, but the worldly character of the Corinthians. The gospel was still the power of God unto salvation to everyone who believed, to the Jew first and also to the Greek (Rom. 1:16).
3. Paul was not afraid to confront the Corinthians regarding their sin, but it was always for their edification (2 Cor. 12:19).

1 Cor. 16:6 | *Paul's Travel Plans Were Circumstantial*

And it may be that I shall come to you and stay with you, or even spend the winter with you, so that you may have the opportunity to send me forth on my journey wherever I decide to go.

Note that the Apostle Paul, in spite of all his unselfish saintliness, did not set his plans with certainty, for he remained flexible. It is stubborn and opinionated people who determine to do something and leave no room for the Lord to intervene and perform His will. Paul was not such a person.

"And It May Be That I Shall *Come to You*"

In the Greek language, Paul begins this verse with the preposition *prós* (4314), toward, which is distinguished from *sún* (4862), conjointly with, or *metá* (3326) meaning "with," "in your company." *Prós* denotes that Paul had something to take up with the Corinthians which he planned to discuss with them.

The Greek word translated "it may be" is *tuchón*, the accusative singular neuter second aorist active participle of *tugchánō* (5177), to happen, to chance. Certainly the Apostle Paul did not presume to know the future nor how circumstances would develop which might permit him to go to Corinth. In 1 Corinthians 4:19 he said, "But I will come to you shortly, if the Lord will." Paul did not adhere to the Greek notion of *túchē* (n.f.), luck, nor the Roman idea of good fortune. There is no doubt, however, that Paul believed that even as a Christian he could not absolutely determine the future, for he qualified his remarks with "it may be."

Why did Paul use the word *tuchón* for "may be" which in its present active participial form is found only in 1 Corinthians 16:6? Certainly it is not because he believed in the Greek goddess *Túchē*, chance. It is to be noted that the word "happiness" in Greek is *eutuchía* (n.f.), and the word "bad luck" or "bad fortune" is *dustuchía* (n.f.). Neither of these words is found in the New Testament, for fortune and misfortune are not delegated to the whims of the Greek mythological deity *Túche*. Another word in Greek that means "happiness" or "prosperity" is the word *eudaimonía* (n.f.). The prefix *eu* (2095), well or good, means "good" in both *eutuchía* and *eudaimonía*, and together they mean happiness. *Eutuchía* means the good favor of the goddess *Túchē,* whereas *eudaimonía* means blessed by the demons (*daímones* [1142], the plural of demon, meaning the aggregate of the Greek mythological gods). Again, neither word occurs in the New Testament; only the noun *deisidaimonía* (1175), translated "superstition," occurs in Acts 25:19. This is the state of respecting and worshiping out of fear what one considers to be a god. It is derived from the verb *deídō* (n.f.), to fear, and the noun *daímōn*, demon. When Paul, in Athens, called the idolatrous Athenians *deisidaimonestérous* (1174), the accusative plural masculine comparative adjectival form of *deisidaímōn*, reverencing an idol representing false deity, he diagnosed the exact state of their attitude. They made idols which they thought represented deity and then they were terrified of them. Then fearing lest they had missed a deity, they made an altar dedicated to the "unknown god" (Acts 17:22, 23).

Knowing Paul's revulsion about the fear of the gods and worshiping idols out of fear, he could not possibly have meant *eudaimonía*, blessedness by the demons. By using the word *tuchṓn*, "may be," he is not indicating that his visit to Corinth could be relegated to the good pleasure of the goddess *Túchē*, but to the true God, the Creator of everything that is in heaven and on earth (Acts 17:24). Paul did not believe in a whimsical god whom no one knew. He believed in the one true God, Jesus Christ, who enters all mankind who believe on Him. The Lord Jesus did not come as a mad demon, but as sent by a living, heavenly Father. The first prayer that the Lord taught His disciples to say was, "Our Father who art in heaven."

"And Stay with You, or Even *Spend the* Winter with You"

Paul believed in the providence of God, but also in prudent planning. Prudent planning takes into account the providence of God that arranges circumstances to fit the execution of His will. This is why in 1 Corinthians 4:19 when Paul said, "I will come to you shortly," he added the most essential belief in the providence of God by saying, "if the Lord will." He planned to go to Corinth and stay for a period of time until he accomplished the tasks he had in mind, but over and above his plans, he superimposed the will of God which was unknown to him. When the God of the universe who ordains everything is our own heavenly Father, we are not afraid to plan and submit those plans to His sovereignty. A child of God submits his plans in absolute faith in his Lord's providence. Thus, 1 Corinthians 16:6 should be studied in conjunction with 1 Corinthians 4:18, 19.

The Lord never taught indecisiveness, for that would rob man of the peace of heart that he needs so desperately in order to accomplish anything. Did you ever notice Christ's command in Luke 12:29: "Neither be you of doubtful mind"? This is translated from *mḗ* (3361), the relative "not," and *meteōrízesthe*,

the second person plural present passive imperative of *meteōrízō* (3349), to suspend one's self in the air, like an uncontrolled meteor. God does not want His children to be drifting like meteors, but to be solidly grounded. At the same time, they must be aware that He can shake the ground underneath them for reasons He alone knows.

Now while Paul believed that it was prudent for him to visit Corinth and perhaps even to spend the winter, yet he was quick to declare that this was his human plan which God could alter. In fact, in 2 Corinthians 1:15–24, he defends the change of plans which God ordained. Likewise, let us plan carefully, but do not forget that we serve a sovereign God who will see to it that His plans are executed, for they take precedence over our own.

"To stay" is expressed with the verb *paramenō̃*, the first person singular future active indicative of *paraménō* (3887), to remain with. It is derived from the preposition *pará* (3844), with, denoting proximity, and *ménō* (3306), to remain, stay.

The preposition *pará*, beside, constitutes the prefix of the two compound verbs (*paramenō̃*, shall stay with, and *paracheimásō* [3914], to spend the winter with) and designates close proximity. Paul expressed his plan and desire to perhaps stay with them and also spend the winter with them. Whether this materialized or not we do not know.

"So That You May Have the Opportunity to Send Me Forth on My Journey"

The expression of this wish of Paul is introduced by the conjunction *hína* (2443), so that, for the purpose of. We have translated the verb *propémpsēte* as "to send forth." It is the second person plural aorist active subjunctive of *propémpō* (4311) which is derived from the preposition *pró* (4253), before, and *pémpō* (3992), to send, dispatch. *Propémpō* in those days meant to send forward on one's journey or take someone on their way. To accompany someone for some distance was a token of respect and honor (Acts 20:38; 21:5). It generally meant to help one forward on his journey (Acts 15:3; Rom. 15:24; 1 Cor. 16:6, 11; 2 Cor. 1:16; Titus 3:13; 3 John 6). Paul, on his part, maintained friendly relations with the Corinthians and looked forward to their expressions of kindness in his visit to Corinth.

"Wherever I Decide to Go"

That his plans were not definite after his visit to Corinth for the second or third time (2 Cor. 1:15; 12:14; 13:1) is evident. *Poreúōmai*, I go, is the first person singular present middle deponent subjunctive form of *poreúomai* (4198), to go. Wherever he was to go, the Corinthians would have the opportunity to give him a farewell and to send him forth with the blessing of God.

LESSONS:

1. Paul was a man who trusted divine providence but who planned his course so that others might know what he was going to do.
2. The word *tuchṓn* should not be taken to mean that Paul believed in luck, for he believed that he should submit his plans to the sovereign will of God (1 Cor. 4:18, 19).
3. Traveling in the winter in Paul's day was hazardous. One should carefully read the troubles that he had on his journey to Rome when he was taken there as a prisoner. He did not plan that trip (Acts 27:16), but, nevertheless, was under God's loving care.
4. Paul wanted to give every opportunity to the Corinthians to show kindness to him. He had evidently written a rather severe letter to them, a letter which appears to have been lost, and he wanted to show that he harbored no ill will toward them (1 Cor. 5:9; 2 Cor. 1:23; 2:1; 3:1; 7:8, 9).

1 Cor. 16:7 | *God's Will Is the Best Will*

For I do not wish to see you now as if I were passing by, but I hope to remain with you for some time if the Lord will permit it.

Paul's primary interest was in the people of Corinth rather than the city itself, especially those who responded to the gospel as a result of his first visit (Acts 18:1–17). Although he suffered persecution in the beginning of his ministry, he had the opportunity of seeing Crispus, the chief ruler of the synagogue, saved. Crispus was replaced by Sosthenes (1 Cor. 1:1) who unsuccessfully tried to silence Paul by bringing him to court under Gallio. However, Paul's behavior in court resulted in Sosthenes' salvation, for we find Paul referring to him as "the brother."

"For I Do Not Wish to See You Now as if I Were Passing By"

Paul did not want this visit to Corinth to be merely a passing visit, but one which would afford him time with the believers there. Although he is entirely resigned to the will of the Lord, he does not hesitate to express his desire in an unwavering manner by stating *ou* (3756), the absolute "not"; *thélō* (2309), will, wish, desire, implying active volition and purpose. It shows that this is his determination in planning, although perhaps the Lord would change the actuality. Paul was not a man whose word was unreliable, but he was a man whose plans could change in view of the needs of others and the guidance of God.

We have translated the word *árti* (737), an adverb of time, as "now." This adverb leads us to believe that Paul may have made a second visit to Corinth which had been short in duration (2 Cor. 12:14; 13:1). Bible scholars are uncertain about this.

The expression *en paródō*, the dative singular feminine of the noun *párodos* (3938), a passing by, is derived from the preposition *pará* (3844), by or through, and *hodós* (3598), road, way, journey. This is the only time that this word is used in the New Testament. Paul longed to spend productive time with the Corinthians.

"But I Hope to Remain with You for Some Time"

The expression *prós humás* (*prós* [4314], toward you, indicating initiative and purpose; *humás* [5209], the accusative plural of the second person personal pronoun *sú* [4771], you) occurs in verses 5 and 6 and now in 7. Paul indicates that a mere passing visit would not suffice, and as far as he was concerned, he wanted to arrange for a longer one. Paul's first visit consisted of a ministry of eighteen months (Acts 18:11). It was around A.D. 53, and the short visit he alluded to, not mentioned specifically in Acts but implied in this verse and in 2 Corinthians 12:14; 13:1, must have been during the years A.D. 54 to 57. In these verses Paul speaks of an intended third visit to Corinth which coincides with that in Acts 20:2. He spent three winter months there (1 Cor. 16:6) in A.D. 57 and 58 during which he wrote the epistle to the Romans (Acts 20:2, 3; Rom. 16:1). Through this phrase "with you" or "toward you," he expresses affection for the Corinthians. This is the visit he intimated in 1 Corinthians 11:34 when he said, "And the rest will I set in order when I come."

The expression "with you" (*prós humás*) has three verbs used in connection with it here in verses 5, 6, and 7. In verse 5, we have the verb *eleúsomai*, I shall come, the future of *érchomai* (2064), to come; in verse 6, the verb *paramenō̃*, shall stay with you, the future of *paraménō* (3887), to stay near; and here in verse 7 the verb *epimeínai*, the aorist active infinitive of *epiménō* (1961), to remain, derived from *epí* (1909), upon, in, at, and *ménō* (3306), to stay or remain. Paul's purpose was to be near the Corinthians, to be among them and to remain there to encourage them in the faith and to discuss with them and set in order the things which yet remained unclear. As we know, the Corinthian church was a wealthy and worldly church, and evidently Paul understood that he could not help them develop into full maturity of the faith in only a few short days or even weeks.

"If the Lord Will Permit It"

The suppositional conjunction "if" is *eán* (1437), the conjunction of reality and experiential possibility. Many times we make plans, as we should, but somehow the Lord does not permit their execution. We must not deny His Lordship over the circumstances of life. We should make our human plans always in the context of God's will. It is not always Satan who cancels the Christian's plans. It is so easy to say I had such and such a plan, but Satan interfered. That is how Paul and his companions must have felt when they were not permitted to proceed with their plans after they had gone through Phrygia and the region of Galatia (Acts 16:6). Notice that the Scripture does not say that Satan stopped them, but that they "were forbidden of the Holy Ghost to preach the Word in Asia" (Acts 16:6). The verb translated "were forbidden" is *kōluthéntes,* the nominative plural masculine aorist passive participial form of *kōlúō* (2967), to hinder, forbid, which is the exact antonym of *epitrépō* (2010), to permit, allow. The Holy Spirit knew what He was doing, for He wanted Paul to preach the gospel in Macedonia. Had it not been for that hindrance to the execution of Paul's plan, perhaps we would not be reading the Word of God and would not be Christians at all.

The Textus Receptus, from which the King James Version was translated, has *epitrépē*, the third person singular present active subjunctive of *epitrépō*. This implies that God will always intervene if He does not want our plans to be executed, although they are meant well. The United Bible Society text, however, has *epitrépsē*, the third person singular aorist active subjunctive. This implies that God would intervene sometimes in a particular cancellation or delay of a certain plan, as in this case. It is always proper for God to intervene when He sees that a plan either delayed or canceled will accrue more effectively for His glory and His honor. We must, therefore, submit our plans, executed in the limited wisdom that we have, to His plans which are enveloped in wisdom and knowledge that are infinite. It behooves us always to make our plans and submit them to God by saying, "if the Lord wills" (*thelḗsē* [2309]; 1 Cor. 4:19; James 4:14, 15).

Every one should plan, but his plans must be underscored, even as was Christ's, that "not my will, but Thine, be done."

LESSONS:

1. Paul desired to minister among the Corinthians, and he made plans accordingly.
2. Paul knew that his plans could be altered at any time as the Lord willed.
3. It is not always Satan who changes our plans; it may be God Himself (Acts 16:6).
4. We should always submit our plans to God's permissive will; His will is far superior to ours for He is omniscient.
5. Any changes Satan may make in our plans are subject to God's permission (Job 1:10–12, 2:2–7).

1 Cor. 16:8 | *Paul's Plan to Remain in Ephesus*

Then I shall remain in Ephesus until Pentecost.

As to when Paul wrote these words, we can only surmise that perhaps it was at the time of the celebration of the resurrection of the Lord Jesus. This would apply especially if we take the "now" of 1 Corinthians 15:20 literally as well as argumentatively: "But **now** is Christ risen from the dead, and become the firstfruits of them that slept." The resurrection of the Lord Jesus occurred during the week of the Jewish Passover known in Greek as *páscha* (3957), and in Hebrew *pasach* (6453, OT), to pass over, spare. The Passover was an exemption, an immunity (Sept.: Ex. 12:11, 21). This great sacrifice and festival of the Jews was instituted in commemoration of God's sparing the Jews when he destroyed the firstborn of the Egyptians. It was celebrated on the fourteenth day of the month of Nisan.

In a wider sense, *pasach* also included the seven days of unleavened bread or the Paschal Festival (Matt. 26:2; Mark 14:1; Luke 2:41; 22:1; John 2:13, 23; 6:4; 11:55; 12:1; 13:1; 18:39; 19:14; Acts 12:4). The Feast of the Passover was also called the Feast of the Unleavened Bread (*azúmōn* [106], without *zúmē* [2219], leaven, a symbol of sin; see Ex. 23:15; Luke 22:1). In Acts 12:3; 20:6 we have reference to the "days of unleavened bread." We have indications that the feast was faithfully and rigidly kept. It was an outstanding season, and so much more for the Christians since the resurrection of the Lord Jesus occurred at the same time.

"Then I Shall Remain in Ephesus"

Paul uses the verb *epimenṓ*, the first person singular future active indicative of *epiménō* (1961) which has as its prefix the preposition *epi* (1909), on, upon, thus meaning in addition to what he was then doing. This is why the figurative meaning of the verb is "to insist." The verb thus has a dual meaning, a literal one and a metaphorical one as used by Paul. He decided to remain in Corinth because there was reason for it. When he was writing this, he was either in Ephesus or near it.

"Until Pentecost"

The word "Pentecost" occurs only in Acts 2:1; 20:16 and in 1 Corinthians 16:8. In Greek it means the fiftieth day (*hēméra* [2250]). Pentecost, therefore, became the feast of the fiftieth day which was commonly known as the Feast of Weeks (Ex. 34:22; Deut. 16:10). Pentecost was also called the Feast of Harvest (Ex. 23:16) or, in Exodus 34:22, the Feast of the Firstfruits of the wheat harvest. In Numbers 28:26 it is called the Day of Firstfruits. It was the feast which marked the conclusion of the harvest (Lev. 23:36; Num. 29:35). This was a feast in which all the Jews in Jerusalem, in addition to devout men out of every nation, came together in Jerusalem to celebrate (Acts 2:5). It was on that day that the Holy Spirit demonstrably came upon the Christians assembled in Jerusalem in the upper room.

Paul indicates here that he wanted to extend his stay in Ephesus from the Feast of the Passover, which was celebrated by believers as the resurrection of the Lord Jesus (Rev. 1:10), through the fifty days that were to follow. Pentecost, then, here appears not as a reference to a Christian feast day but merely to denote a period of time (Acts 20:16). Later, in the Christian calendar, Pentecost became a feast celebrating the visible coming of the Holy Spirit fifty days after the resurrection of the Lord Jesus.

<u>LESSONS</u>:

1. Paul indicates his plan to stay in Ephesus for a particular period of time.
2. He indicates that period of time circumscribed by great events in the history of the world as pertaining to the Jewish calendar and as demonstrated by the divine activity in and through Christ.
3. The two great events that Paul uses to circumscribe the time were the resurrection of the Lord Jesus and the demonstrative coming of the Holy Spirit (1 Cor. 15; Acts 1:2, 5; 2:1–13).

1 Cor. 16:9 | *Seizing Every Opportunity*

For a great and effective door has been opened to me, and there are many adversaries.

Paul was sensitive to the opportunities that were his and his alone and those which were available for all. Likewise, we must be especially sensitive for the personal opportunities that God gives us and ask the Lord for definite guidance.

"For a Great and Effective Door"

The word *gár* (1063), for or because, indicates the reason why Paul wanted to stay for a period of time in Ephesus, and it becomes evident in the opportunity expressed by the word *thúra* (2374), door. It is noteworthy, however, that the word "door" has no definite article in front of it. In Acts 14:27, 1 Corinthians 16:9, 2 Corinthians 2:12, Colossians 4:3 and Revelation 3:8; 4:1 whenever the word "door" is used without the article, it refers to a specific opportunity. Paul does not make plain just what the opportunity was, but simply that it had been opened and that it was great (*megálē*, the nominative singular feminine of the adjective *mégas* [3173], great). Paul perceived that this was an extraordinary situation which God was presenting to him, and he should be present in Ephesus to utilize it.

What we have translated as "effective" is the Greek word *energḗs* (1756), efficient, energetic, the nominative singular feminine adjective derived from the preposition *en* (1722), in, and *érgon* (2041), work, energy, capable of making something happen. It is accomplishing the work or purpose it is supposed to accomplish. *Energḗs* is an adjective corresponding to the noun *enérgeia* (1753), energy, efficiency. The exact opposite would be *adráneia* (n.f.), inactivity. *Enérgeia* is that which enables one to move on and accomplish what he set out to accomplish. That which results from *enérgeia*, energy, is called *enérgēma* (1755). *Energḗmata* is translated in the King James Version as "operations" (1 Cor. 12:6), "workings" (1 Cor. 12:10), and "effective" here in verse 9. We also find it translated "effectual" in Philemon 6: "That the communication of your faith may become effectual [*energḗs*] by the acknowledgment of every good thing which is in you in Christ Jesus." Here Paul is encouraging Philemon that the communication of his faith is productive and effective, and, therefore, it is a faith worth every effort. It occurs also in Hebrews 4:12 where it says, "For the Word of God is quick and powerful [*energḗs*] and sharper than any two-edged sword, piercing even to the dividing asunder of soul and spirit, of the joints and marrow, and is the discerner of the thoughts and intents of the heart." Thus, the Word of God is active, able to penetrate any heart and mind and, therefore, should be communicated unhesitatingly with all rejection of any thought of ineffectiveness.

"Has Been Opened to Me"

The first thing that Paul recognized was that this door was not opened by him, but by Someone other than himself, which is to be taken as the Lord. The verb is *anéōge* which is the third person singular perfect active indicative of *anoígō* (455), to open. The perfect tense indicates that someone opened it in the past and it remains open, but the assumption is that Paul does not know how long it will remain open. The active indicative mood demonstrates that this opportunity was given solely by the active will of God, without the necessary assistance of anyone. The Lord opened the door, and thus it was Paul's imperative duty to enter. The personal responsibility that Paul had to enter the door is demonstrated by the word *moí* (3427), unto or for me, dative singular first person of the personal pronoun *egṓ* (1473), I. This was a door of opportunity that the Lord presented to Paul directly to take advantage of that which may not have been available to others.

The only other occurrence in Scripture where we find the words *thúra*, door, and *moí*, to me, used together is 2 Corinthians 2:12 where Paul says, "Furthermore, when I came to Troas to preach Christ's gospel, and a door was opened unto me of the Lord." The Greek word translated "was opened" is *aneōgménēs*, the genitive singular feminine perfect passive participial form of *anoígō*, to open. It is evident that this opportunity was given to Paul by the Lord Himself.

What is the door that Paul calls "great and effectual"? We are not told, but we shall do well to carefully study Acts 19:8–41 and try to determine what is meant by this expression. We are not told when the various events during Paul's stay in Ephesus occurred chronologically. In 1 Corinthians 16:5, Paul expresses his desire to come to the Corinthians, and in verse 6, he expresses a desire to stay with them for a while. In Acts 19:22, however, we find that instead of going personally to Macedonia and, consequently, we presume, to Corinth, he sent Timothy and Erastus, "But he himself stayed in Asia for a season." This agrees with the verse of this chapter, 1 Corinthians 16:9, in which he says he is going to stay in Ephesus for a period of time because a great door which is effective was open to him. He knew his ministry would produce results as he proclaimed the gospel to the Ephesians.

When Paul ministered in Ephesus, however, we read in Acts 19:23–41 that a riot broke out. This came about because of the devotion which the Ephesians had to the cult of Artemis by which they were distinguished. In verse 31 we read of a group of people which are called "certain of the chief of Asia" in the King James Version. In the original Greek, it speaks of them as the *Asiárchai* (775), derived from *Asía* (773), Asia, and *árchō* (757), to rule. The people of whom Paul speaks and who had positions of leadership in Ephesus were apparently called "rulers of Asia." All research into who they were leaves us with only conjectures. Some have ventured to say that they were leaders elected into an honorary and complimentary position in a kind of parliament that had some unknown role in the affairs of Ephesus at the time that Paul was there. The principal duty of the president of this body was to supervise the worship of the emperor in Rome and throughout the province where Ephesus was located. This province was known as Asia Minor. In the years just prior to Christianity finding an entrance into Ephesus and Asia Minor, which the Romans called Asia, there was a conflict between the particular worship of Diana and what came to be known as "emperor worship" introduced by Attalus the Third, the king of Pergamus in 133 B.C. Some presume that the Asiarchs mentioned in Acts 19:31 were leaders favoring the cult of emperor worship versus the local worship of the goddess Diana or Artemis. There may have arisen a conflict between fidelity to a local deity and fidelity to the worshiping of the emperor which was promoted in Pergamus (Rev. 2:12–17).

In Acts 19:31 we are told, "Even some of the Asiarchs being his [Paul's] friends, having sent *a message* to him, were requesting him that he should not adventure himself into the theater" (a.t.). These Asiarchs were leaders of the whole province of Asia who, however, in a supernatural intervention of God, became Paul's friends. Perhaps this came about during his stay and ministry in Ephesus where he had observed the Ephesians' total devotion to a local deity. These men sided with Paul and, in doing so, with the Lord who had instructed Paul that a great and effective door was going to be opened in Ephesus. They are called his "friends" (*phíloi* [5384]), meaning those who had the same interests as Paul had.

"And *There Are* Many Adversaries"

This phrase begins with *kaí* (2532), and. It is then followed by *antikeímenoi*, the nominative plural masculine present middle deponent participle of *antíkeimai* (480), to be opposing. The word "many" is *polloí*, the nominative plural masculine adjectival form of *polús* (4183), much.

The Lord had called Paul to delay his departure from Ephesus to perform a particular task. It would not be an easy task, but the Lord entrusted it to Paul. Paul did not accept the challenge blindly, for he knew there were many in Ephesus who were opposed to him and his teachings. In speaking about the opposition which he was going to confront, he uses the milder of two Greek words that can be translated "to oppose." There is the word *anthístēmi* (436) meaning to stand against, to resist. Then there is the word *antíkeimai* which is used here which indicates milder opposition. This has the same preposition *antí* (473), against, but the verb is *keímai* (2749) which means to lie, to be placed, thus meaning to lie or be placed against something. So it does not necessarily mean to stand and fight, but to hold an opposing view which may not be belligerent. The verb *antíkeimai* is more inclusive in that it may include both those opposing passively and actively. However, both categories indicate opposition, for they both have the prefix *antí* with the meaning of "against." Some may oppose sitting down (*keímenoi*), whereas some oppose standing, ready to fight. Ephesus was a city even more idolatrous than Corinth where the goddess Diana was greatly venerated. Here they built a temple dedicated to Diana which was so elaborate and great that it was considered one of the seven wonders of the world. Nevertheless, it is recorded that in Ephesus, "God wrought special miracles by the hands of Paul" (Acts 19:11). It was also in Ephesus that the Holy Spirit acted so powerfully that "Many of them [among the opposing ones] also which used curious arts brought their books together and burned them before all *men*: and they counted the price of them and found it 50,000 *pieces* of silver" (Acts 19:19). Although there were many who opposed Paul and his teaching in Ephesus, yet "mightily grew the Word of God and prevailed" (v. 20). So Paul was able, in spite of the opposition of many, to win some of the Asiarchs, the provincial rulers, who became his friends and stood by him. But in spite of all the uproar at the great theater of Ephesus which held 24,000 people, Paul was finally freed and set sail for Macedonia and ultimately Corinth.

It is also noteworthy to discern who presented the greatest opposition to Paul in Ephesus. It was those who were able to profit from the religious instincts of the people. One such person was a man by the name of Demetrius, a silversmith, who made silver shrines for Diana, which brought no small gain to the craftsmen (Acts 19:24). He vehemently objected to Paul's preaching because he knew that the Christian faith would bring an end to his craft and profiteering which took advantage of the ignorance of the people. These craftsmen in Ephesus knew that the true God whom Paul was preaching would destroy their business of manufacturing little gods and idols (vv. 25–28). Those whose pocketbooks are hurt as a result of the preaching of the true God are the ones most likely to vehemently oppose the gospel just as there are those who will attach themselves to the body of Christ for personal profit.

LESSONS:

1. Paul recognized that God had opened a great and effective door in Ephesus for him to enter.
2. Paul knew that it was not going to be easy, but in spite of the anticipated opposition, he decided to heed the call of God and enter the door and use the opportunity afforded to him.
3. He wanted to tarry in Ephesus in spite of the fact that he had to delay his coming to Corinth. Sometimes when we heed the call of God other things have to suffer.
4. There are some who will strongly oppose the gospel if it is going to hurt their profits just as there are some who will embrace it for personal advantage.
5. While recognizing the adversaries, Paul wisely chose to enter the door God had opened for him.

1 Cor. 16:10 — *God's Workers Are Worthy of Honor*

Now if Timothy comes, see to it that he may be without fear in your midst, for he works the work of the Lord as I also.

Paul was determined to obey God and stay in Ephesus to do the work appointed to him by the Lord, but he thought it proper to send Timothy to Corinth.

"Now if Timothy Comes"

Probably no one among Paul's coworkers was closer to him than Timothy, his child in the faith, as he called him (1 Cor. 4:17; 1 Tim. 1:2, 18; 2 Tim. 1:2). By referring to Timothy as "his child," Paul may have meant that he had a part in his conversion or in his instruction in the faith. We see Timothy appear on the scene as Paul crosses into Greece. Not only is he found in the company of Paul, assisting him, but we find him sent on different missions by Paul (Acts 17:14, 15; 18:5; 19:22; 20:4; Rom. 16:21; 1 Cor. 16:10; 2 Cor. 1:19; Phil. 2:19; 1 Thess. 3:2, 6). When trouble broke out in Corinth, we find Paul thinking of sending Timothy to the Corinthians as his own worthy representative. In 1 Corinthians 4:17, 18 he writes, "For this cause have I sent unto you Timothy, who is my beloved son, and faithful in the Lord, who shall bring you into remembrance of my ways which be in Christ, as I teach everywhere in every church. Now some are puffed up, as though I would not come to you."

Our verse begins with the suppositional conjunction *eán* (1437), the "if" of reality and possibility. This shows that Timothy was with Paul in Ephesus at this time. This may be the instance referred to in Acts 19:21, 22; 2 Timothy 1:15, 18. Timothy, with others who represented the Macedonian churches, took part in the organizing of the collection for the church at Jerusalem, but it does not seem that he accompanied Paul in taking it there (Acts 20:4, 13–16).

"See to It"

Since there was the real possibility that Timothy would go to Corinth, Paul wanted to make sure that he was properly received. Therefore, he says to the Corinthians, "See to it" [*blépete*, the second person plural present active imperative of *blépō* {991}, to see, to heed]. Since Timothy was a young man, it is conceivable that the Corinthians would not give him the proper respect due him.

"That He May Be Without Fear in Your Midst"

"That he may be" is the verb *génētai*, the third person singular second aorist middle deponent subjunctive of *gínomai* (1096), to become, to be. Paul was concerned that on this occasion of Timothy's visit the Corinthians would intimidate him and make him afraid. Perhaps Paul expected the Corinthians to treat Timothy the way they had treated him when in 1 Corinthians 2:3 he said, "And I was with you in weakness, and in fear [*phóbō*, the dative of *phóbos* {5401}, fear which is in the adverb *aphóbōs* {870}, without fear, as used by Paul here in 1 Cor. 16:10], and in much trembling." If the Corinthians with their behavior could arouse fear to the point of trembling in Paul, how much more in young Timothy! In writing to the same Corinthians in 2 Corinthians 5:11, Paul said, "Knowing [*eidótes*, the nominative plural masculine perfect active participle of *eidō* {1492} which means receiving or knowing as a result of a relationship with Christ, and not *ginṓskontes* {1097}, knowing experientially by being taught], therefore, the terror [*phóbon*, fear] of the Lord, we persuade men; but we are made manifest unto God; and I trust also are made manifest in your consciences." Paul intimates here that we Christians should fear God and not men, for the fear of God produces holiness (2 Cor. 7:1). It seems that the fear Timothy might experience in Corinth was not the fear engendered by the enemies of the gospel, but by the conduct of the believers themselves (2 Cor. 7:5). Apparently, Paul had to send a very severe letter to the Corinthians, and this caused him much sorrow (2 Cor. 7:8), but we gather that in the end, Paul sent Titus as a substitute for Timothy (2 Cor. 7:13–15).

For the fourth time, the expression *prós humás*, to or toward you, occurs in this passage (vv. 5–7). In English this is better translated "in your midst." How shameful that the Apostle Paul found it necessary to admonish the Corinthians to treat Timothy properly when he was among them.

"For He Works the Work of the Lord as I Also"

Paul wanted the Corinthians to understand that Timothy would not have any other reason to come to Corinth except to serve the same Lord as he did also. He wanted Timothy to be accepted in his stead, for all of God's workers are worthy of honor and respect.

LESSONS:

1. Paul considered it necessary to send a personal representative to Corinth.

2. Since Timothy was working with Paul in Ephesus and since Paul was eager to enter the door that the Lord was opening for him there, he thought of sending Timothy to Corinth.
3. Paul wanted to forewarn the Corinthians not to intimidate Timothy as he dealt with their problems.
4. The fear of man should not intimidate the servant of God.
5. Paul wanted to make sure that the Corinthians understood that Timothy did not have his own agenda, but that he would deal with the difficulties he encountered there the same as Paul would.
6. Can we be trusted to carry out the task, even in the face of difficulties, that God has given us to do?

1 Cor. 16:11 | *God's Servants Should Not Be Despised*

Therefore let not anyone despise him, but send him forth in peace, so that he may come to me, for I am expecting him with the brothers.

Christians, through their critical attitude, may many times frustrate the holiest of ambitions by saintly leaders in God's service, such as Paul and Timothy.

"Therefore Let Not Anyone Despise Him"

Paul shifts his advice from the plural "you take heed" (*blépete* [991]) to the singular, "let not anyone" (*mḗ* [3361], the relative "not"; *tis* [5100], anyone, the nominative singular masculine indefinite pronoun). Each of the Corinthians should take heed lest they intimidate Timothy, and not one of them should despise him. All it takes in a church is one person to express a negative evaluation about somebody else to cause trouble. That is the meaning of the word *exouthenḗsē*, the third person singular aorist active subjunctive of *exouthenéō* (1848), to despise, disdain. The verb is derived from *ek* (1537), used as an intensive, and *outhenéō*, from *outheís*, the *oudeís* (3762), nobody. The verb means to bring to naught, to despise, to treat with scorn or throw out as nothing (Luke 18:9; 23:11; Rom. 14:3, 10; 1 Cor. 1:28; 6:4; 16:11; 2 Cor. 10:10). It is to be disdained as worthless. If that was the treatment that Timothy was going to experience among the Corinthians, it could not be expected that he would be able to settle problems among them. For anyone to be successful in resolving problems, a good measure of respect and honor must exist for the mediator. Apparently, that was not the treatment that Timothy found among the Corinthians, and so at a later time, Paul sent Titus to them (2 Cor. 7:6, 7; 12:17, 18). However, this was not Paul's first choice for them.

"But Send Him Forth in Peace, so That He May Come to Me"

The verb in this phrase is *propémpsate*, the second person plural aorist active imperative of *propémpō* (4311), to send forth, which verb is used in verse 6. Evidently, the Corinthians did not send Timothy forth in peace because one person began to find fault with him, and consequently others joined in and despised both him and his ministry among them.

The verb *exoutheneō* is stronger than the synonym *kataphroneō* (2706), to hold in contempt, think lightly of, or to look down upon. *Kataphronéo* is only in one's mind, while *exoutheneō*, to make contemptible, despicable, or to appear as nothing, is an activity beyond a personal thought. It means to make others feel and act in the same way. The Corinthians sent Timothy back feeling worthless and that he had failed in his mission, and they made their attitude evident by their actions. The text implies that the whole process started with one person despising Timothy. Attitudes are contagious.

"For I Am Expecting Him with the Brothers"

How eagerly Paul expected Timothy back with good news. The verb *ekdéchomai* (1551) means to await with eagerness, to expect, to look forward to. The experience of sending Timothy to Corinth brought great disappointment to Paul's heart because he had such great expectations from this mission.

Paul was not the only one expecting Timothy back in peace. There must have been other believers who, along with Paul, sent him on his mission to Corinth. "With the brothers" must mean the brethren who sent Timothy to Corinth and undoubtedly followed him with prayer, awaiting his return. However, the obstinacy and fault-finding of the Corinthians totally disappointed them. How quickly the expectation of believers can be frustrated by the contemptibility of people such as the Corinthians who do not care what grief and trouble their attitude toward others brings.

LESSONS:

1. Paul implies that the mission of Timothy ultimately failed because someone from within the Corinthian church showed a contemptible attitude toward him.
2. Evidently Timothy returned from Corinth discouraged and depressed, thinking himself a failure, when in reality, it was the Corinthians who had failed to show the proper respect and honor.
3. The Corinthians may have prided themselves over their possession of spiritual gifts, but they should rather have been humbled by their spirit of disdain for the Lord's servants.

1 Cor. 16:12 — Discerning the Opportune Time

And concerning brother Apollos, I besought him much to come to you together with the brothers, and it was not his desire to come now, but he will come when he has opportunity.

Paul had sent young Timothy to Corinth to help them through some of their difficulties. He was not well received. In fact, he was disdained and evidently returned to Paul dejected, having his self-esteem destroyed. In this verse, we now find that Paul very much wanted Apollos to go to Corinth, but he refused.

"And Concerning Brother Apollos"

Apollos was an Alexandrian Jew who came to Ephesus where Acquila and Priscilla instructed him in the way of the Lord. Although his knowledge about the Lord Jesus was not complete, he accepted His Messiahship knowing only the baptism of John (Acts 18:25, 26; 19:1–6). A Christian church had not yet been established in Ephesus, but after Paul's return from Corinth to Ephesus, some Christians welcomed Apollos in Corinth (Acts 18:27, 28). In Acts 18:24, 25, 28 we read that Apollos was an eloquent man, fervent in the spirit, teaching the Word of the Lord diligently, and mightily convincing the Jews that Jesus was the Christ. The word of Apollos' visit in Corinth is described as "helping them much which had believed through grace" (Acts 18:27). Apollos, then, was much esteemed among the Corinthians to whom he taught grace. Apollos is presented as having watered the field in the sowing and planting of the Word of God in Corinth (1 Cor. 3:6). He must be recognized as the man who built on the foundation that Paul had laid (1 Cor. 3:10, 11). Paul speaks of Apollos as a tutor, while he presents himself as a father to the Corinthians (1 Cor. 4:15). Apollos, then, ministered more as an instructor or teacher of the Word of God among the Corinthian Christians than as an evangelist. He was highly learned (*lógios* [3052]), a man of reflection and words and a great orator who knew what he was saying. This was not said of anyone else. In fact, he became so well-accepted that an "Apollos following" arose in Corinth (1 Cor. 1:12).

Paul may not have considered Apollos to be among the great Christian teachers in Corinth, as he does not mention his name along with Timothy and Silvanus (2 Cor. 1:19). In Titus 3:13, Paul mentions him in conjunction with a lawyer by the name of Zenas, but he does not extol him in extraordinary terms.

"I Besought Him Much"

Since Apollos was so highly esteemed by the Corinthians, it seems Paul wanted him to go there to see what he could contribute to solving their problems, but Apollos did not accept Paul's invitation. Probably he was not in Ephesus at the time that Paul asked him to go to Corinth.

For the fifth time in this chapter, Paul uses the expression *prós humás*, to you (*prós* [4314], to; *humás* [5209], you; see also vv. 5–7, 10), as if to indicate that the Corinthian Christians were constituting the problem and not the worldly environment of the city of Corinth.

Paul affectionately calls Apollos "the brother," in spite of the fact that the Corinthians had instituted a party in his name. For this, however, Apollos may not have been responsible at all, and in 1 Corinthians 3:1–9, we find that Paul did not lay blame on him for the party that arose in his name. As Paul was not responsible for the party that bore his name, Apollos could not be held responsible for the "Apollos party." Paul considered him his coworker in Corinth, and he realized that his work there in watering the ground was as valid as his own in planting the seed (1 Cor. 3:5–8). He considered Apollos and himself as fellow workers in God's vineyard. Paul's attitude toward Apollos was, indeed, exemplary, and he was neither envious of him nor critical. This is the reason why, at this time, it was his choice to send him to Corinth.

Paul earnestly entreated Apollos to go to Corinth. The word "much" is *pollá*, the plural of the neuter adverb *polús* (4183), "much" as to quantity. It is not many times, but much in intensity which could not be expressed with the singular *polú*. The verb *parekálesa* is the aorist of *parakaléō* (3870), to beseech, request. Had it been a repeated request, it would have been in the imperfect tense *parekaloúmen*. The way it is expressed in the aorist, however, speaks of the manner in which Paul requested Apollos to go to Corinth. Although Paul was an apostle and he asserted his apostleship among the Corinthians (1 Cor. 9:1), he did not in any way command Apollos to go to them. Paul assumes no hierarchical function in his relationship even with a coworker (1 Cor. 3:9). *Parakaléō* is the sweetest and most gentle verb that Paul could have used. Some verbs that carry the connotation of a command are *diastéllomai* (1291), to enjoin; *diatássō* (1299), to order; *entéllomai* (1781), to charge, command; *epitássō* (2004), to conscript; *keleúō* (2753), to order; *paraggéllō* (3853), to give orders; *prostássō* (4367), to arrange toward, bid or order that it be so. Any of these words would have been a stronger word than *parakaléō*, to beseech or request, which the Apostle used. We find this word used on a number of occasions when people turned to the Lord Jesus for help (Matt. 8:5; Mark 1:40; 5:18; 6:56; 8:22; Luke 7:4). The "beseeching," however, of Paul in asking Apollos to go to Corinth had an urgency to it.

"To Come to You Together with the Brothers"

All that Paul wanted was that Apollos go to the Corinthians to convey his heart to them. This is translated from *hína* (2443), in order that; *élthē*, the third person singular second aorist active subjunctive of *érchomai* (2064), to come. The message Paul wanted Apollos to convey to the Corinthians is expressed in the words of 2 Corinthians 6:11–13. A simple translation can hardly convey what the original Greek entails. Let us try to paraphrase it:

> Our mouths have been opened to you [the Corinthians] to express how our hearts have been opened wide to receive you. You should not feel sorry for us, but you should feel sorry for how we have been treated in your inner affections. As to my children I speak, let us have equal treatment by widening your hearts of love toward us.

This, if it were possible to adequately translate it, would interpret how Paul felt toward the Corinthians, for he did not experience the same love from them that he held for them in the very depths of his heart. Paul wanted Apollos to convey this message in the presence of other brothers who were to go from Ephesus with him.

"And It Was Not His Desire to Come Now"

Since Paul pled much with Apollos to go to Corinth and convey his heartfelt feelings, Apollos' refusal must have added to Paul's grief.

The unwillingness of Apollos to go to the Corinthians at the request of Paul was resolute. This is expressed by the adverb *pántōs* (3843), wholly, altogether, by all means, surely (Luke 4:23; Acts 18:21; 21:22; 28:4; Rom. 3:9; 1 Cor. 5:10; 9:10, 22).

And apparently Paul did not try to intimidate Apollos into accepting his request as an apostle's order to perform this duty. Paul allowed Apollos to exercise his own judgment and his own agenda, for he knew that God in His omniscience worked together all things for good (Rom. 8:28).

Apollos' refusal is expressed by the phrase *ouk* (3756), the absolute "not"; *ḗn*, the third person singular imperfect indicative of *eimí* (1510), to be; *thélēma* (2307), an accusative singular neuter of the noun meaning "will." The imperfect tense should be noted here. This was not Apollos' own determination to refuse to go at the bidding of Paul, but it was **not** the will of God for him to go to Corinth at the time requested. We are not told why Apollos made that determination, but obviously God was in it.

When the Apostle Paul speaks of *thélēma*, will, he does not specify whose desire or choice determined Apollos' refusal to go to the Corinthians. Whereas we have translated this as if it were Apollos' desire not to go at the time that he was requested, it is to be noted that in every other instance in the Corinthian Epistles where the word *thélēma* is mentioned, the designation is "of God" (1 Cor. 1:1; 2 Cor. 1:1; 8:5). An exception to this is 1 Corinthians 7:37 where it has an entirely different meaning, that is, a desire which refers to lust. Apollos' decision, therefore, was a personal judgment which was different from Paul's, and he had the courage to let Paul know his mind.

Here are two servants of Christ: Paul the apostle and Apollos, whom Paul calls a fellow worker of the Lord (1 Cor. 3:9), one who does an important work for the Lord equal to his own (vv. 5–8). Yet we find that they disagree as to the going and coming in the work which they are conducting.

This diversion of wills was not the only time Paul experienced disagreement with fellow workers. He was forsaken by John Mark who returned to Jerusalem (Acts 15:38). On the island of Cyprus, John Mark served Paul and Barnabas as a servant (*hupērétēs* [5257], a servant who does menial work). But later, when Paul and Barnabas planned to take another journey, Barnabas, who was an uncle to John Mark, wanted to take Mark with them. Paul objected, and Barnabas and Mark went together to Cyprus while Paul and Silas went together through Syria and Cilicia (Acts 15:36–40). In verse 39 we find that the contention (*paroxusmós* [3948], provocation, paroxysm) was sharp between Paul and Barnabas concerning Mark. Differences of opinion can characterize individuals in the pursuit of their work for the Lord, but there should arise no criticism nor bitterness between those who disagree, as there was no bitterness in Paul when Apollos decided not to go to Corinth when Paul requested. This shows us that individuals should exercise their own discernment, for the Lord never deprives his children of personal judgment. And again, when disagreements arise as to God's leading, we must not assume our brother is out of God's will and allow resentment and even hatred to develop. God leads different people different ways, and, like each different piece of a puzzle, at the end they will all fit together to form a pre-planned picture designed by God.

Apollos' refusal was not that he would not go to Corinth at all, but only "at this time" (*nún* [3568], now). This does not mean that he was unwilling to go later.

"But He Will Come When He Has Opportunity"

Paul was not angry nor displeased that Apollos would not go to Corinth when asked, in spite of the fact that he respected Paul. And Paul respected the private, personal leading of the Lord in Apollos' life, not only as to what he should do, but when he should do it. That Paul did not force Apollos to go to Corinth when he wanted him to go is indicated by the phrase under discussion here. The verb is *eukairḗsē*, the third person singular aorist active subjunctive of *eukairéō* (2119), to have opportunity.

It is derived from *eu* (2095), good, and *kairós* (2540), season, opportune time. Thus the meaning is when the opportunity afforded itself for the best results according to Apollos' judgment.

In the Greek New Testament we find two words which express "time." One is *chrónos* (5550), quantitative time or a period measured by the succession of objects and events which denote the passing of moments. The second word is *kairós*, season, the time of accomplishment or the period which may be qualitatively viewed as the best occasion for executing something. We can do anything at any time, but part of the gift of the discernment of God is for man to do what he must do at the opportune time. This is different from convenience. Convenience indicates ease of effort, while opportunity indicates the appropriate time when something should be done, that is, a definite time for a definite task. For instance, there is a season (*kairós*) of harvest (Matt. 13:30). There is only one appropriate time for harvest, and that is when God brings the ripening of the fruit. There is an acknowledgement, then, of a higher power in the season of harvest, and that is the power of God (see Matt. 13:30; Mark 11:13; Luke 20:10). The maturity of a man shows in his recognition of the proper time at which definitive things can be accomplished.

Observe that Paul not only recognizes this as the prerogative of Apollos to choose when to go to Corinth, but he does not presume to know better what is the best time. When we assume the choosing of the time that someone else should do something, we give the impression that he is not mature enough to make a wise choice or that God cannot lead him directly, but only through us. Although Paul was an apostle, he did not want to infringe upon Apollos' freedom to do as he felt the Lord was leading him. The verb *eukairḗsē*, good or opportune time, is in the active voice, meaning that it was the right of the individual to choose for himself. For this reason, Paul only requested

Apollos to go to Corinth when he wanted him to go, but he left the execution of the plan to Apollos' judgment.

LESSONS:

1. Paul does not assume a hierarchical position as an apostle who could order Apollos to go to Corinth whether Apollos wanted to go or not.
2. Apollos exercises discriminatory choice with which he is endowed as an individual.
3. Paul did not criticize Apollos for the establishment of the "Apollos following" in Corinth, as he himself did not want to be blamed for the "Paul following" there (1 Cor. 1:12, 13).
4. He recognizes that Apollos had his particular duty and, along with himself, he considered them as both being workers together with God (1 Cor. 3:5–9).
5. Apollos did not shirk the duty of going to the Corinthians, but simply wanted to go when the opportunity was more appropriate.
6. Even though we may feel strongly that it would be God's will for another person to do something, we must leave that to their judgment and leading of the Lord.
7. It would be sinful on our part to allow resentment or bitterness to develop against anyone just because they are convinced that God is leading them differently than we think best.

1 Cor. 16:13 | *Imperatives for a Victorious Christian Life*

Be alert, continue to stand in the faith, act like men, be established.

The Corinthian church was replete with problems. Paul had sent spiritual leaders and teachers among them with mixed results. He now gives a few final exhortations which are concise but poignant. In simple words, Paul is telling the Corinthian Christians to grow up and behave like men.

"Be Alert"

In closing this epistle, Paul gives four exhortations which indicate that the Christian life is one of constant danger and trouble, and if we are going to be victorious, we must always be alert. This is why we have translated the present imperative *grēgoreíte* (second person plural present active imperative) as "Be alert." A colloquial expression would be "Watch out!" The verb *grēgoréō* (1127), usually translated as "bchold," was a favorite word of our Lord (Matt. 24:42, 43; 25:13; 26:38, 40, 41; Mark 13:34, 35, 37; 14:34, 37, 38; Luke 12:37, 39).

The first use of the verb *grēgoreíte* by our Lord is in relation to His Second Coming. He wants us to be alert in view of the fact that we do not know the time nor the hour when He will come.

Every time that our Lord tells His disciples to be on the alert, it is due to their ignorance of the time of His coming. In Matthew 24:42, the Lord said, "Be alert [*grēgoreíte*] therefore, for you do not know what hour your Lord is coming [*érchetai*, the third person singular present middle deponent indicative of *érchomai* {2064}, to come]." The verb *érchetai*, "He is in the process of coming," is often used to describe the details of His coming and strongly implies, in the context of the NT, that the process or planning of His return has already begun. Another verb that is used with reference to the coming of Christ is *eleúsetai*, "He will come." This verb stresses the fact that He will come.

The Lord Jesus, just before delivering Himself to be crucified, said to His disciples, "I go to prepare a place for you, and if I go and prepare a place for you, I am coming [*érchomai*, in the present indicative, and not *eleúsomai*, I will come] again, and will receive you unto Myself; that where I am, there you may be also" (John 14:1–3). When the believers are taken to be with the Lord, transformed or resurrected, all others are going to be left in the world to experience the Great Tribulation (Dan. 9:25–27; Rev. 6—19).

Matthew 25:31 speaks of the coming of the Son of Man in glory. The verb there is *élthē*, the third person singular second aorist active subjunctive of *érchomai*. This pinpoints His coming as the final coming in His glory; therefore, it says *élthē* and not *érchetai* which we find to be the verbal form in connection with the believers' alertness regarding the sudden coming of the Lord Jesus to take them unto Himself.

The Lord Jesus also admonished His disciples to be on the alert during His time of agony in the Garden of Gethsemane where He was going to be betrayed (Matt. 26:38, 40, 41; Mark 14:37, 38). Who would have expected one of the Twelve, Judas, to betray the Lord Jesus and deliver Him for crucifixion? The disciples had no idea whatsoever that one of their own company would betray their Master, although they should have had from His remarks made at the last supper concerning His betrayal (Matt. 26:21–24; Mark 14:18–21; Luke 22:21–23; John 12:21–30).

Therefore, the first reason for the vigilance of the believer is that the Lord is coming unexpectedly, and some of our closest companions may turn against us. For these two reasons, we should be alert with the sudden expectation of His return as well as the possible betrayal of those in whom we trust.

How Should We Be Alert?

We can find answers to this question in Matthew 26:41 and Mark 14:38. This was Christ's word to His disciples who could not stay awake for an hour in Gethsemane while their Lord was agonizing over His cross. He said to them, "Be alert [*grēgoreíte*] and pray [*proseúchesthe*, the second person plural present middle deponent imperative of *proseúchomai* {4336}, to pray]." The word "pray" here is the general word for prayer to God (*proseuchḗ* [4335]). As we pray to God, we shall keep alert for His coming and we shall be prepared for those who pretend they are our friends, but in reality are our enemies.

In Colossians 4:2, Paul says, "Continue in prayer and watch [*grēgoroúntes*, the nominative plural masculine present active participle of *grēgoréō*] in the same with thanksgiving." The thanksgiving is that we have the Lord in heaven (Col. 4:1) and that we are unafraid. We are vigilant in prayer with thanksgiving remembering that as time goes on, our salvation is closer than before (Rom. 13:11).

Another verb that is closely indicative of our behavior in being alert is mentioned in 1 Thessalonians 5:6 and 1 Peter 5:8. It is the verb *nḗphō* (3525), to abstain from wine and to keep sober, to be discreet. Originally, however, it meant to refrain from drunkenness and to maintain a sense of calmness or coolness, prepared for any emergency. A person who is intoxicated cannot be alert and ready for surprises.

First Thessalonians 5:2, 6 dwells on the suddenness of the coming of the Lord as a thief in the night. It says, "Therefore let us not sleep [*katheúdōmen*, the first person plural present active subjunctive of *katheúdō* {2518}, to slumber or sleep while duty or danger requires that one stay awake] as do others; but let us watch [*grēgorṓmen*] and be sober [*nḗphōmen*]." When someone is drunk or asleep, he certainly is not alert.

First Peter 5:8 says, "Be sober [*nḗpsate*, the second person plural aorist active imperative of *nḗphō*], be vigilant [*grēgorḗsate*, the second person plural aorist active imperative of *grēgoréō*], because your adversary the devil, as a roaring lion, walks about, seeking whom he may devour." If we are not aware of the wiles of the devil, he will find an opportunity to trip us.

In Revelation 16:15, there is the beatitude of alertness:

> Behold I come as a thief. Blessed [*makários* {3107}, blessed, the same word as we find in the Beatitudes in Matt. 5; cf. author's book *The Pursuit of Happiness* on the meaning of the phrase "to be indwelt by God" thus being fully satisfied] is he that watches [*ho,* he; *grēgorṓn,* the nominative singular masculine present active participle of *grēgoréō,* meaning the one who is constantly vigilant or on the alert], and keeps his garment, lest he walk naked, and they see his shame.

This verse tells us that the vigilant person is the one indwelt by God, and the alertness that he exercises in his life is the result of that indwelling. There is no way that the person who is not indwelt by God and fully satisfied because of His presence can be on the alert. Therefore, Paul gives this advice to believers in Corinth who were greatly lacking in spiritual commitment.

"Continue to Stand in the Faith"

The second exhortation that Paul gives to the Corinthians is to "continue to stand [*stḗkete*, the second person plural present active imperative of *stḗkō* {4739}, to stand] in the faith." The verb *stḗkō* is a later verbal form found only in the present tense, evolved from *éstēka*, the perfect tense of the verb *hístemi* (2476), to stand. Since the verb *éstēka* is the perfect of *hístēmi*, to stand, it must give the verb as it is used here a proper association with the perfect form. To render it precisely, it should be stated as "having stood, continue to stand."

This letter to Corinthian believers by Paul is in conclusion of all that he has said to them. This is, so to speak, his last will and testament to them: first, to be alert; and secondly, to realize that they are now standing in the faith because they have taken a stand—they have believed on the Lord Jesus Christ and they were saved. In 1 Corinthians 1:18, Paul says, "For the preaching of the cross is to them that perish foolishness; but unto us which are saved it is the power of God." This translation of the King James Version misses the fact that the Greek says, "to us who are **being** saved" (*sōzoménois*, the dative plural masculine present passive participle of *sṓzō* [4982], to save; see also 2 Cor. 2:15). The Corinthian believers began to stand when they believed on the Lord Jesus Christ and were saved. Paul admonishes them, that having been saved and made to stand in the faith, they should now continue to do so. They were reverting to their old habits of their life of unbelief. Their standing was not now of their own selves, but it was because of the faith they had exercised in Jesus Christ. If it were not for that faith, they would not be standing at all.

The modifier is "in the faith." "Faith" here is *pístei*, the dative of *pístis* (4102), faith. We are, therefore, fully justified to translate the verb *stḗkete* as "to continue to stand" and not just "stand fast" (KJV) since this is the imperative of *stḗkō* which derives from the perfect tense of *hístēmi,* to stand. We stand because of our faith in Christ, and in that faith we continue to stand.

It is noteworthy that there are only three modifiers to the verb "stand." The first is faith. Our verse does not say just "faith," but "**the** faith." This gives a definitive technical meaning to the word *pístis*, faith. As a technical term, it indicates the means of appropriating what God in Christ has for man resulting in the transformation of his character and way of life. Such can be termed the gospel of Christian faith (Rom. 3:22ff.). In Philippians 1:27, it is called "the faith of [or in] the gospel." That means that a man chooses to believe the good news, and that by believing on the work of Christ, man is made to stand upright instead of being dead in his sins and trespasses (Eph. 2:1; cf. 1 Thess. 2:13). Faith does not mean mere persuasion about any matter, but explicit trust in the gospel which is the truth. The gospel and the truth of the gospel have the power to make a man stand. It is called "the faith" in 1 Corinthians 2:5; 2 Corinthians 4:13; Philippians 1:25; 2:17; 1 Thessalonians 1:3; 1 Timothy 3:9; 6:12; 2 Timothy 1:5; 2:18; Titus 1:13; Philemon 6; Hebrews 12:2; James 2:1, and 1 Peter 5:9.

Another modifier, besides "the faith," used with the verb *stḗkete* is "one Spirit." In Philippians 1:27, it says, "Only let your conversation be as it becomes the gospel of Christ: that whether I come and see you, or else be absent, I may hear of your affairs, that you stand fast in one Spirit, with one mind striving together for the faith of the gospel." In the King James Version, the word "Spirit" is with a small "s." I believe it should be a capital "S," thus referring to the Spirit of God, for it is by the Spirit of God that believers are made to stand in the faith and to keep standing.

Besides "the faith" and "the Spirit," we find the modifier "the Lord." In Philippians 4:1, we read, "Therefore, my brethren dearly beloved and longed for, my joy and crown, so stand fast in the Lord, my dearly beloved" (cf. 1 Thess. 3:8). It is only in the Lord, through the power of Him who rules sovereignly indeed, that we have been able to stand in Him and remain standing.

How We Can Know We Are Standing in the Faith

There are certain characteristics and attributes that show our position in Christ, in the faith and in the Holy Spirit. These are shown in a number of Scripture verses that occur with the basic verb *hístēmi,* to stand. In Romans 11:20 we read,

> Well; because of unbelief [*apistía* {570}, absence of faith in Jesus Christ] they were broken off and you stand [*éstēkas,* the perfect active indicative] by the faith. Be not high minded [*hupsēlophrónei,* the second person singular present active imperative of *hupsēlophronéō* {5309}, to think more highly than you ought to, meaning to be proud], but fear [*phoboú,* the second person singular present middle deponent imperative of *phobéō* {5399}, to fear or to respect].

So if we see a person who thinks of himself more highly than he ought and is not respectful of God, we know that person is not continuing to stand in the faith in Jesus Christ and is not inspired by the Holy Spirit.

The second characteristic of the person who stands in the faith is the joy of the Lord in him. Second Corinthians 1:24 says, "For not that we have dominion over your faith, but are helpers of your joy: for by faith you stand" [*estḗkate,* the perfect active indicative]. The person who does not have the joy of the Lord in him does not have the Lord. A person is confident that he stands in the Lord when he knows that he has received something that he did not possess at one time and which has brought salvation to his soul. He knows that he is being saved all the time, and that it is a possession he will never lose.

First Corinthians 15:1–3 states,

> Moreover, brethren, I declare unto you the gospel which I preached unto you, which also you have received [*parelábete,* the second person plural second aorist active indicative of *paralambánō* {3880}, to receive] and wherein you stand [*estḗkate,* the second person plural perfect active indicative of *hístēmi,* to stand]; by which also you are being saved [*sṓzesthe,* the second person plural present passive indicative of *sṓzō,* to save].

Note that it does not say "you **were** saved," but "you **are being** saved." This shows both the initial salvation and the continuation of that salvation.

This verse continues: "if you keep in memory what I preached unto you, unless you have believed in vain. For I delivered unto you first of all that which I also received, how that Christ died for our sins according to the Scriptures." Note the verb *katéchete*, the second person plural present active indicative of *katéchō* (2722), to possess. In the King James Version it is translated "if you keep in memory," but it would be better rendered "if you really possess." That which one receives saves him, and he knows it, and he knows that his salvation is not of self (Eph. 2:8–10). It is the believer's possession (John 3:16–18), and his confidence in that possession in Jesus Christ is another characteristic of standing in the faith.

Another characteristic of the person who is standing in faith is that he knows his access to God and regularly takes advantage of that privilege. Romans 5:2 says, "Through whom also we have had [*eschḗkamen*, the first person plural perfect active indicative of *échō* {2192}, to have] access by faith into this grace wherein we stand, and rejoice in hope of the glory of God."

The grace in which we stand is genuine and true because it has worked a change in our conduct and restores us in our hopelessness as 1 Peter 5:12 says: "I have written briefly, exhorting and testifying that this is the true grace of God wherein you stand." The "true" here means genuine (*alēthḗ* [227], true as opposed to false [*pseudḗs* {5571}]). True grace, when received, changes a man's conduct entirely, and this change is discernible by others.

He who stands is not deceived. In 1 Corinthians 10:12, we read, "Wherefore let him who thinks he stands [*hestánai*, the perfect active infinitive of *hístēmi*, to stand] take heed lest he fall." This verse has nothing to do with salvation, but with the proper estimate of one's strength in tackling the problems of life of which there are many.

The Christian stands in the faith when he struggles for other Christians. Colossians 4:12 speaks of Epaphras, the minister of the Colossian church: "Epaphras who is one of you, a servant of Christ, salutes you, always laboring fervently for you in prayers, that you may stand [*stḗte*, the second person plural second aorist active subjunctive of *hístēmi*, to stand] perfect and complete in all the will of God." We can know that a person stands in the faith when we see him helping others.

A Christian stands when he uses the available armor of God. Ephesians 6:11 says, "Put on the whole armor of God, that you may be able to stand against the wiles of the devil." He realizes that Satan is alive and active in the world and that he does not have to fight against him bare-handed, but with the armor God makes available. The Christian must learn to resist so that when he meets opposition, he will prevail. Ephesians 6:13 says, "Wherefore take unto you the whole armor of God, that you may be able to withstand [*antistḗnai*, the second aorist active infinitive of *anthístēmi* {436}, to resist] in the evil day, and having done all, to stand [*stḗnai*, the second aorist active infinitive of *hístēmi*]."

Where could we find a better example of a man who stood in the faith than Paul? When he stood before King Agrippa, he told him first how wicked he had been and how he had imprisoned the Christians after receiving authorization from the chief priests to do so (Acts 26:8–11). But then he told the king how the risen Christ had appeared to him from heaven and said to him, "Stand [*stḗthi*, the second person singular second aorist active imperative of *hístēmi*] upon thy feet" (v. 16). In verse 23, he explained that the power of his standing in the faith was the resurrection of Jesus Christ. Indeed, a person who has true faith in the crucified and risen Christ shows every evidence that he stands in the faith by not thinking of himself higher than he should, by fearing God, by the joy of his salvation, by the possession of the grace of God, by the access he has to God, and by knowing that His grace is genuine because of the change it has wrought in his life. The Christian who stands in the faith is not self-deceived, for he fights with the full armor of God against the devil and other evil forces. He has the example of Paul who has withstood the devil and the evil in the world because of the resurrection of Jesus Christ.

"Act Like Men"

The third imperative that Paul uses is *andrízesthe*, the second person plural present middle deponent imperative of *andrízō* (407), to behave as a man with the wisdom and courage of a mature person as opposed to a baby, occurring only here in 1 Corinthians 16:13. The exact opposite of our verb is *nēpiázō* (3515), to be or to act as a baby. *Nēpiázō* occurs only in 1 Corinthians 14:20, where reference is made to the mental maturity of an adult compared to a baby. The verse says, "Brethren, be not children in understanding: howbeit in malice you *must* be infants [*nēpiázete*, the second person plural present active imperative of *nēpiázō*, to be and to act like an infant], but in understanding be men" [*téleioi*, the plural of *téleios* {5046}, one reaching his or her goal].

By using the verb *andrízesthe*, Paul is telling the Corinthians to be and act like mature men who have the physical and mental ability to be victorious in the struggles and battles of life. We will reach our goal if we act like men and not babies.

"Be Established"

The last of the imperatives is *krataioústhe*, the second person plural present passive imperative of *krataióō* (2901), to make strong. In order to arrive at the specific meaning of the verb *krataióō*, which is translated "to be strong," we must examine the noun *krátos* (2904), dominion or establishment that prevails. In Modern Greek *krátos* means an established government or prevailing order. Paul's command to "Be alert, continue to stand in the faith, be and act like mature men," implies that the believer is established in the recognition that he has the power that will prevail because it is of God, that his foundation is firm (1 Cor. 3:10, 11). *Krátos* stands as a synonym of two other words that mean strength. One is *ischús* (2479), inherent strength, and the other is *dúnamis* (1411), accomplishing power. There is yet another word for strength which is *enérgeia* (1753), active power (see ch. 9).

The dominion of the Lord is an eternal dominion (1 Tim. 6:16; 1 Pet. 4:11; 5:11; Jude 1:25; Rev. 1:6; 5:13). In 1 Corinthians 16:13, there is a progression in the state of the believer as expressed in the four verbs of our verse under study. He becomes alert, he continues to stand in the faith, he is and acts with maturity, and he is established in the kingdom of God. The verb *krataioústhe* is in the passive voice which means that he is established by Someone other than himself. That Someone, of course, is Jesus Christ to whom is ascribed "eternal dominion" (*aiṓnion* [166], eternal; *krátos*) as in 1 Timothy 6:16, in the King James Version translated "power."

In Ephesians 6:10 we find that this dominion or establishment is achieved through the inherent power of God: "Finally, my brethren, be strong [*endunamoústhe*, the second person plural present passive imperative of *endunamóō* {1743}, to strengthen] in the Lord and in the dominion [*krátos*] of His might [*ischús*]." Here we find the Apostle Paul implying that the inherent might (*ischús*) of God enables the believer to accomplish (*dúnamis*) the establishment of His dominion (*krátos*), and this establishment is achieved through the Holy Spirit (Eph. 3:16). What a promise! What a challenge!

LESSONS:

1. The Christian should be alert insofar as the sudden and unknown time of the coming of the Lord is concerned.
2. A believer should be alert insofar as the attacks of the devil are concerned.
3. One who believes in Christ should be prepared to resist evil as he realizes that he lives in a sinful world.
4. The believer should also understand that his feet are on a firm foundation and that he should build upon it (1 Cor. 3:10–13).
5. The Christian should not be a crybaby, but be mature in his mind.
6. A believer should realize that he is established through the inherent and accomplishing power of the Holy Spirit.

1 Cor. 16:14 | *Faith Should Be Exercised in Love*

Let all things pertaining to you be done in love.

In verse 13, through the four imperatives—be on the alert, continue to stand in the faith, act like men, and be established—we are reminded that as Christians we are to be alive and active. The believer must not be half-dead, or almost dead, nor should he be asleep. Christ vitalizes and invigorates, and, experiencing the faith that is in Christ, we have also experienced His love (1 John 5:1).

"Let All Things *Pertaining to* You"

In Romans 14:7, Paul tells us that no one lives unto himself. The life that we have in Christ through faith should make us unselfish. Paul demonstrates in his discussion of the life the Christian should choose to live, that there are others to consider in the body of Christ in addition to those who are without the body. Those who are in the body of Christ should not be despised nor offended, but should be accepted in the performance of their particular function in the body.

"Be Done in Love"

As for those who are without the body of Christ, Paul showed his commitment to win as many as possible to Christ (1 Cor.

9:19). His concern, then, here in 1 Corinthians 16:14, is that our faith should not be practiced with ourselves only in mind. He says, "Let all things *pertaining to* you be done in love." The adjective *pánta*, the accusative plural neuter adjectival form of *pás* (3956), everything, is followed by the personal pronoun *humṓn* (5216), yours. In our translation, we elucidated by adding "*pertaining to*." This has the same meaning which we find in Romans 12:18: "If it be possible, as much as lies in you, live peaceably with all men." In whatever you do, as far as you are concerned, let it be done in love.

The verb used here is *ginésthō*, the third person singular present middle deponent imperative of *gínomai* (1096), to be, become. The present imperative indicates that this is not just one particular thing done by you, but that everything, irrespective of time, should be done in love. This is the Christian way of life that Paul recommends. Let us elaborate on this in a practical way in each area suggested by the imperatives of the previous verse.

The first one is, "Be alert. . . but do it in love." We saw that the verb *grēgoreíte* (1127) is used by our Lord mostly in relation to His coming to receive the believers unto Himself. It is as if Paul were saying, Be alert in the expectation of your Lord, but let it be in love.

I refer the reader to my exposition of 1 Corinthians 1:8 in my book entitled *A Richer Life for You in Christ*. There I pointed out that the coming of our Lord Jesus Christ refers both to the Day of the Lord, which to the unbelievers will be a day of reckoning or a day of judgment, and also to the rapture of the church. The Rapture is the day of Jesus Christ when He will descend from heaven and take His children unto Himself. While the coming of the Lord will be an ecstatic experience for His saints, for the unbelievers who remain behind to experience the Great Tribulation, it will be a dreadful one. So for the believers, the coming of the Lord is a joyful event, but at the same time one enveloped in sorrow for those who will remain behind. As we look with great expectancy to our Lord's return, we must also show our tender concern for those who will remain behind and for whom the coming of the Lord will be as a thief in the night (1 Thess. 5:2). While the believer lives in hope, yet he should be lovingly concerned for unbelievers and the retribution their unbelief will bring upon them.

Secondly, the believer is to continue in the faith. He experiences a firmness and stability on the one foundation which is Jesus Christ. However, as he is resisting the devil and the evil in the world, he is experiencing spiritual and moral maturity. All the time, he sees unbelievers who are living in a state of defeat and swallowed up by the world. So his firmness in victory must be in love and prayer for the unbelievers who do not have our wonderful hope.

Also, as we believers establish our dominion in the kingdom of God, we are to act like men and not be weaklings. We must look with pity on unbelievers who are being tossed about in the sea of uncertainty. Our heart should be courageous and daring in our desire to save them.

As the roots of a tree are established, they extend themselves and the tree grows and becomes more firmly grounded, and the tree that has roots brings forth fruit. The love that should characterize the believer should be one that extends itself. There is an adjective in Greek that the translators have been unable to express correctly, and that is the adjective *ektenḗs* (1618), which comes from the verb *ekteínō* (1614), to stretch out, to extend. The love of the Christian, therefore, should be characterized as extending love, reaching out to all, including unbelievers whom we see missing the joy believers experience. Certainly, while we are enjoying the victories of faith here on earth and in the expectation of heaven, we should always be consumed by love for all, both believers and unbelievers.

LESSONS:

1. Love expressed by the Apostle Paul is not human love, but divine love, as delineated in 1 Corinthians 13.
2. Divine love is expressed as a result of the indwelling of God in the human heart.
3. It is unselfish love, the appropriation of God's love that motivates an unselfish love for others.
4. This love should govern all the believer's actions and relationships, since we are far richer than the wealthiest unbeliever, and we owe it to them to share what Christ has given us.

1 Cor. 16:15 — Volunteers in the Ministry

Now I beseech you, brothers (you recognize that the family of Stephanas is the initial fruit of Achaia, and that they properly placed themselves in the ministry to the saints), . . .

In verse 12, Paul spoke of requesting Apollos to go to Corinth, which he declined to do at that time. Again, in this verse, we find Paul using the same verb in his request to the Corinthians.

"Now I Beseech You, Brothers"

We pointed out in verse 12 that the word *parakalṓ* from *parakaléō* (3870), to beseech, was the most polite word that Paul could have used in making a request. Paul is gentle and polite in his dealings with the Corinthians and does not in any way display pressure or authority in his request, although he was an apostle.

"You Recognize That the Family of Stephanas Is the Initial Fruit of Achaia"

The first thing we need to examine is who Stephanas is. Apparently he believed on the Lord Jesus Christ as a result of the preaching of Paul in Achaia, a region to which both Athens and Corinth belonged. Most probably he came to the Lord in

Athens. Paul calls him "the initial fruit" (*aparchḗ* [536], firstfruit, meaning the beginning of fruitbearing with other fruit to follow [Rom. 8:23; 11:16; 16:5; 1 Cor. 15:20, 23; 16:15; James 1:18; Rev. 14:4]).

The first mention of the name Stephanas is in 1 Corinthians 1:16 in which Paul tells us that he baptized him and his household or family (*oíkon*, the accusative of *oíkos* [3624], metonymically meaning household, those who live together in a home [Luke 10:5; Acts 10:2; 11:14; 16:15; 1 Cor. 1:16; 2 Tim. 1:16; Titus 1:11]). The word *oíkos*, besides being used for "house" in the sense of a structure, represents the family in its widest sense (Acts 2:46; 8:3; 20:20). The family may include father, mother, children, near relations, and dependents as used in the New Testament of Pharaoh (Acts 7:10) and of Cornelius (Acts 10:2; 11:14); of the Philippian jailer (Acts 16:31); of Crispus (Acts 18:8); of Stephanas (1 Cor. 1:16); of the bishop (1 Tim. 3:4); of the widow (1 Tim. 5:4); of Onesiphorus (2 Tim. 1:16; 4:19), who apparently was dead and whose household nevertheless bore his name; of Noah (Heb. 11:7); of deacons (1 Tim. 3:12), and of Christians generally (Titus 1:11). *Oíkos* also meant the descendants (Luke 1:27; 2:4).

Whereas 1 Corinthians 1:16 mentions Stephanas' household (*oíkon*, the accusative of *oíkos*), here in 1 Corinthians 16:15 it says *oikían*, the accusative of *oikía* (3614). There is generally a difference between these two words. *Oíkos* had a broader range than *oikía* and refers to the whole estate, whereas *oikía* is simply one's residence and only occasionally does the word include its contents. But in these two texts, the words are used synonymously and are far more inclusive. In 1 Corinthians 1:16, it speaks of the members of the family of Stephanas who were baptized by the Apostle Paul himself, while our verse under examination speaks more generally of the dedication not only of the family of Stephanas, but of the commitment of all their belongings to the ministry of the gospel. Stephanas and his family were like the first believers at Pentecost who, according to Acts 4:32, were characterized by selflessness: "And the multitude of them that believed were of one heart and of one soul: neither said any of them that aught of the things which he possessed was his own; but they had all things common." That was a voluntary commitment, not only of themselves, but of all that belonged to them. What a wonderful example!

The Stephanas family constituted an exception in that they were baptized by Paul personally which was not his custom (1 Cor. 1:17). It was a distinct privilege to be baptized by the great Apostle.

Having recognized the dedication and commitment of Stephanas' household, Paul requests the brethren to recognize in Stephanas' family the same commitment that he recognized.

The grammarians and the exegetes are puzzled as to whether *oídate* is an indicative or an imperative. If it is an indicative, it is the perfect of the verb *eídō* (1492) which is used with present meaning, that is, "you do recognize." If it is in the imperative mood, it means "you should or must recognize." Does Paul tell the Corinthians to recognize that Stephanas' family was totally committed to the Lord, or does he simply recognize the commitment to the Lord of their household, including all their possessions. It is noteworthy that the verb *oídate* is never used in the New Testament as an imperative, but always as an indicative. Therefore, I feel it should be taken here as used the same way. In such a case, Paul is telling the Corinthian believers that since the Stephanas' family was completely committed to the Lord, having placed themselves in their appropriate niche of service in the local church, they gave themselves to the ministry to the saints. In other words, if we accept *oídate* in the indicative mood, we must treat it as the participle *eidótes*, recognizing. Thus the Stephanas family's complete commitment to the Lord in what they were and what they had explains their generosity.

First of all, Paul knows that the Stephanas family was the firstfruit (*aparchḗ*) of his evangelistic effort in Achaia. In other words, all the members of this family were believers as were the first believers at Pentecost and of whom nothing more complimentary could have been said than they did not consider their possessions as their own (Acts 4:32). These people brought their possessions and laid them at the feet of the apostles (Acts 4:34, 35; see also Acts 2:44, 45).

"And That They *Properly* Placed Themselves in the Ministry to the Saints"

The Apostle Paul confirms that genuine faith resulted in the household of Stephanas appropriately placing themselves in the service of the ministry to the saints.

There is no doubt that the ministry in the local church at Corinth was not appointed to this family by anyone in the fellowship. Rather, the Stephanas family discerned what needed to be done, and they did it. We translated the verb *étaxan*, the third person plural aorist active indicative of *tássō* (5021), to set in order, arrange, as "*properly* placed." The object is *heautoús*, themselves, the accusative plural masculine third person of the reflexive pronoun *heautoú* (1438), himself. This means that they had discernment regarding the needs of the local church and consequently analyzed their talents accordingly so that they could fit themselves in where they could best serve the saints.

What we translated as "ministry" is *diakonía* (1248). This implies passionate love to the needy within the Christian community (Acts 6:1, 4; 2 Cor. 8:4; 9:12, 13; Rev. 2:19). It is an effort to benefit others in their greatest need.

Ministry and Ministering

In the Greek New Testament, the idea of ministering and ministry is found in six groups of words:[1]

The first is *diákonos* (1249), minister, a deacon; *diakonía*, ministry; and *diakonéō* (1247), to minister. These are general terms of Christian service. There were those in the congregation who detected the needs of others and tried to discern their own talents and abilities to meet those particular needs. The Christian church at the time of writing the New Testament was not organized into local entities wherein the word "minister" was used with the same sense as we use it today. *Diákonos*, minister, is found in Matthew 20:26; 22:13; 23:11; Mark 9:35; 10:43; John 2:5, 9; 12:26; and in the Pauline Epistles in Romans 13:4 (twice); 15:8; 16:1; 1 Corinthians 3:5; 2 Corinthians 3:6; 6:4; 11:15 (twice), 23; Galatians 2:17; Ephesians 3:7; 6:21; Philippians 1:1; Colossians 1:7, 23, 25; 4:7; 1 Thessalonians 3:2; 1 Timothy 3:8, 12; 4:6. In the Gospels, it is rendered as "servant," and in the Epistles as "minister," except in Philippians 1:1 and 1 Timothy 3: 8, 12 where it is rendered "deacon."

Diakonía or ministry occurs in Luke 10:40; Acts 1:17, 25; 6:1, 4; 11:29; 12:25; 20:24; 21:19 and in all groups of the Pauline Epistles (Rom. 11:13; 12:7; 15:31; 1 Cor. 12:5; 16:15; 2 Cor. 3:7–9 (twice); 4:1; 5:18; 6:3; 8:4; 9:1, 12, 13; 11:8; Eph. 4:12; Col. 4:17; 1 Tim. 1:12; 2 Tim. 4:5, 11). The only epistles where it is not found are Galatians, Philippians, 1 and 2 Thessalonians and Titus. The usual translation is "ministry," although "ministration" is found in 2 Corinthians 3:7-9; 9:13; "ministering" in 2 Corinthians 8:4; 9:1; "relief" in Acts 7:29, and "serving" in Luke 10:40. It is also found in Hebrews 1:14 and Revelation 2:19.

[1]For a discussion of these words, see author's *Complete Word Study Dictionary: New Testament* under *hupēretéō* [5256], to serve under the direction of another.

The verb is always translated "to minister" in Matthew and Mark, and nearly always the same in the Epistles. In John it is "to serve." In Luke and Acts both translations are used, but "to serve" is used most frequently. The service in the office of deacons is expressed as "to serve as deacons" (1 Tim. 3:10, 13).

The second group of words is *doúlos* (1401), a servant who, however, is related to the master as a slave and who must, at all times, be subservient. The noun is *douleía* (1397), bondage, and the verb is *douleúō* (1398), to serve as a bond slave.

The third group is *hupērétēs* (5257), attendant, subordinate, assistant, servant; and *hupēretéō* (5256), to serve as a subordinate or as a sailor on a ship. The noun *huperesía*, which is not found in the New Testament, means service under the direction of someone.

The fourth is *latreía* (2999), ministration as rendered to God and referring to worship that includes service and service that includes worship; *latreúō* (3000), to minister, render religious homage, worship, and at the same time, service.

The fifth group of words is *leitourgós* (3011), public servant, an official of the church or state; *leitourgía* (3009), a public function as that of a priest from which comes the word "liturgy," a public ministry which includes both worship and service; *leitourgéō* (3008), to be a public servant, perform religious or charitable functions, to minister by worshiping God and serving man, and *leitourgikós* (3010), ministering.

The sixth group of words is *therápōn* (2324), a menial attendant who shows heart concern; *therapeía* (2322), attendants, domestic servants, cure, healing which includes heart and emotional concern; *therapeúō* (2323), to wait upon menially, heal, and at the same time, show concern. This is the word from which the English "therapeutic" is derived.

Godly Determination

The word that is used to describe the household of Stephanas is *diakonía*, which means to meet the needs of other people with whatever means one has. This family was determined to meet the needs of the church in Corinth in whatever way they could, including physical service with everything they had at their disposal. It is to be noted that their ministry was first and primarily to the saints within the church, but it also included Christians everywhere. As Paul says in Galatians 6:10, "As we have therefore opportunity, let us do good unto all men, especially unto them who are of the household of faith."

LESSONS:

1. The family of Stephanas had a special place in the heart of Paul. Not only did he baptize them personally, but he calls the attention of the believers in Corinth to their example of service.
2. Paul could proudly point to the Stephanas family and say that they were in the worthy tradition of the first believers who were saved at Pentecost, who, without any prompting, volunteered their own possessions and had them in common with others (Acts 2:44; 4:32).
3. This family did not wait to be appointed to render service, but they appointed themselves to serve in whatever capacity was needed. They were true volunteers.

1 Cor. 16:16 | Volunteers Deserve Cooperation and Respect

So that you, also, ought to subject yourselves to such and to everyone who cooperates and works hard.

The verb *étaxan* in the previous verse, which we translated "they *properly* placed themselves," comes from the verb *tássō* (5021), to set in order, to arrange appropriately. The word *hupotássō* (5293), to place under in an orderly fashion, comes from this verb also. The preposition that serves as a prefix is *hupó* (5259), under. The family of Stephanas volunteered to use all they had to meet the needs of others as they discerned them. The Apostle Paul commended their dedication and now gives some advice to the Corinthians in view of such an example.

"So That You, Also, Ought to Subject Yourselves to Such."

"So that" translates the conjunction of purpose *hína* (2443). The conjunction *kaí* (2532), also, should not be omitted as in some translations. If the family of Stephanas volunteered to meet whatever need existed, others should follow their example, too. Thus the apostle advises the Corinthian church to properly place themselves under (*hupotássēsthe*, the second person plural present passive subjunctive of *hupotássō*, to subject) that family in respect to their example.

"And to Everyone Who Cooperates"

Respect and cooperation is owed to such people and also to those who have tried to help them. "Cooperates" is the participle *sunergoúnti*, the dative singular masculine present active participle of *sunergéō* (4903), to cooperate, from the preposition *sún* (4862), conjointly together, and *érgon* (2041), work. Thus we have a verb meaning to work closely together. It is God's will and command that we work together as a team.

"And Works Hard"

There is also another verb in this verse relating to work. It is *kopiṓnti*, the dative singular masculine present active participle of *kopiáō* (2872), to work hard and become tired as a result. Corresponding to the verb *kopiáō* is *kópos* (2873), toil, labor, fatigue. Both words come ultimately from *kóptō* (2875), to strike.

In Revelation 2:2, 3, the Lord said to the angel of the church at Ephesus, "You have patience, and for My name's sake you labored and did not faint" (MT). The verb for this last expression is *ouk* (3756), the absolute "not," and *ekopíasas*, the second person singular aorist active indicative of *kopiáō*, to work hard. Thus together these two words mean not to give up as a result of fatigue that comes from hard work. Our Lord will not forget the hard work we have done for Him and will reward us accordingly.

These two participles, *sunergoúnti* and *kopiṓnti*, are both in the present tense which shows the commendation that goes to the person who is always cooperating and working hard. This attitude should characterize believers who want to do something for their Lord. If people took seriously Paul's advice to respect those who voluntarily work for the Lord and to become coworkers with them, not for the ease of the task, but for the glory of God, there would be a spiritual revolution in the Christian church. This is in contrast to the easy pace that characterizes so many in their work for the Lord.

<u>LESSONS</u>:

1. Those who labor for the Lord voluntarily ought to become our example and provide leadership which we are advised to follow.
2. We should be characterized by a spirit of cooperation at all times.
3. Do not seek the easy task, but one that involves effort, and God will reward accordingly.
4. When you work, be willing to work to the point of exhaustion, knowing that your work will not go unnoticed.

1 Cor. 16:17 — *Filling the Void in Another's Life*

I rejoice over the coming of Stephanas and Fortunatus and Achaicus because they filled a void which you could not fill in your absence.

In the previous two verses, Paul spoke of the household of Stephanas and commended their good work for the Lord. In this verse, we are given a little more information regarding this man named Stephanas.

"I Rejoice over the Coming of Stephanas and Fortunatus and Achaicus"

These three men constituted a delegation which the church in Corinth sent to the Apostle Paul while he was in Ephesus. Perhaps they brought a letter to him asking questions concerning marriage (1 Cor. 7:1ff.). Originally, Paul had written to the Corinthians as a result of hearing from the household of Chloe that there were disputes in the church. Paul now expresses his joy over the coming of these three men by using the verb *chaírō* (5463), the first person singular present active indicative meaning to rejoice. We have no information as to how long these men stayed in Ephesus nor whether they carried back a letter from Paul.

The word that is used for their coming and presence with Paul is *parousía* (3952) which has the combined meaning of "coming" and "presence." This word became a technical term used for the coming again of Christ (Matt. 24:3; 1 Cor. 15:23; 1 Thess. 2:19; 2 Thess. 2:8; 2 Pet. 3:4; 1 John 2:28).

The only one of these three men that we have any information about is Stephanas. He is first mentioned in 1 Corinthians 1:16 as having been baptized by Paul. He, along with his household, are also mentioned in 1 Corinthians 16:15 as being the firstfruits of Paul's labor in Achaia which was the region where Corinth was situated. Fortunatus was probably of Roman origin because he has a Roman name, and Achaicus was probably one of the believers in Corinth. We are told nothing about them.

"Because They Filled a Void Which You Could Not Fill *in Your Absence*"

Paul speaks of these three men as having filled a void of some kind. This is expressed by the verb *aneplḗrōsan*, the third person plural aorist active indicative of *anaplēróō* (378), to fill the place of someone or something (cf. 1 Cor. 14:16). We are not told specifically what this void was. It may have been a physical need which Paul had, or it may have been a need for fellowship and encouragement in the work, although by reading verse 18 which follows, we tend to believe it was the latter. Whatever it was, it met the need of Paul and proved a blessing to him. Paul would have been delighted if he could have been in the presence of all the Corinthian believers, but since this was impossible, the presence of these three men filled the lack and the need which Paul was experiencing. We, too, can be used of the Lord in meeting the needs of our fellow Christians in various ways when we make ourselves available to Him.

LESSONS:

1. In spite of the fact that Paul could not find much to praise the Corinthians about (1 Cor. 11:22), yet he rejoiced in the work that the Holy Spirit had done in Corinth, and it was a joy for him to have evidence of it by the coming of these three men.
2. Paul's deep love and concern for the Corinthians was obvious when he wrote in 1 Corinthians 4:15 that he was like a father to them.
3. His advice to the Corinthians was not condemnatory, but corrective and redemptive as a father's advice should be.

1 Cor. 16:18 | Recognize Those Who Bring Spiritual Rest

They brought rest both to my own spirit and to yours; therefore recognize such ones.

The three representatives of the Corinthian church not only filled the void that existed in the heart and spirit of Paul from not being able to see the Corinthians and enjoy their fellowship, but they did something by their very presence that was beneficial to Paul.

"They Brought Rest"

The word used here by the Apostle Paul is *anépausan*, the third person plural aorist active indicative of *anapaúō* (373), to rest, relieve, refresh. This compound verb is derived from *aná* (303), again, and *paúō* (3973), to cease, give rest. The noun is *anápausis* (372), rest. Both the verb and the noun, however, represent that inner tranquility which is primarily given by the Lord Jesus Christ.

This rest is not merely a cessation of work and the renewal of physical strength, but that inner calmness which comes from the quietness given by the divine Spirit. *Anápausis* is the word used to express the inner rest that God, basically and primarily, gives to the sinner who is heavy laden: "Come unto Me all you that labor and are heavy laden, and I will give you rest [*anapaúsō*, the first person singular future active indicative of *anāpaúō*] . . . and you shall find rest [*anápausin,* the singular accusative feminine of the noun a*nápausis*] unto your souls" (Matt. 11:28, 29).

Two other words that are synonymous with *anépausan* are the verb *katapaúō* (2664), to settle down or to rest as a result of stoppage from work, and the noun *katápausis* (2663), the rest that comes from cessation of work. These are derived from the preposition *katá* (2596), an intensive meaning "down," and *paúō*, to make to cease. He who comes to Christ does not find his rest in the cessation of work or in a state of settling down, but finds inner tranquility in spite of hard labor and subjection to physical fatigue. Those who come to Christ find not only salvation, but an inner peace that passes all understanding (Phil. 4:7). The enigma of a saved Christian is how he can experience both physical fatigue and a quiet restful spirit at the same time. This is a gift of God which comes through faith.

What Jesus Christ basically does when He saves the sinner, we as believers can also do for other believers in our ministry to them. It is in this sense that Paul wrote that the three representatives from the Corinthian Church brought rest or refreshment to his spirit as also to the spirit of the saved Corinthians.

In Luke 12:13–21, we have our Lord's parable of the rich, foolish farmer. He thought he could find his inner peace through the abundance of material things which he gathered for himself. He erroneously said to his soul, "Soul, you have much goods laid up for many years; take your ease [*anapaúou*, the second person singular present middle imperative of *anapaúō*, have inner peace], eat, drink, and be merry." No wonder the Lord called him a fool, for he should have known that food and drink and material things do not satisfy the soul. Only the Spirit of God can satisfy the immaterial part of man, the soul/spirit. Once the Spirit of God effects this spiritual transformation in man's spirit, there is regeneration, the new birth from above (John 3:3, 7). Then when a person's spirit is regenerated, the fellow members of the body of Christ (1 Cor. 12:13) can bring refreshment (*anápausis*) to the already regenerated spirit, but not that original inner peace which only Christ gives to the sinner. This is what the New Testament calls *paráklēsis* (3874), encouragement, comfort, and *parēgoría* (3931), consolation, comfort, from which the English word "paregoric" is derived. Paregoric is a preparation which soothes and calms the stomach.

The rest which Christ brings to the sinner does not enable him to live in the world without personal stress and trouble. In fact, it was to His disciples that the Lord Jesus said, "These things I have spoken unto you, that in Me you might have peace [a synonym of *anápausis*]. In the world you shall have tribulation; but be of good cheer; I have overcome the world" (John 16:33). We as believers can either enhance this basic peace given by the Lord, or we can disturb it. The Corinthians must have disturbed their own inner tranquility and that of the Apostle Paul often because they were acting as babies, as carnal and not as mature believers (1 Cor. 3:1–4). Paul appraised the situation realistically and honestly, and he rebuked when necessary for the purpose of the Corinthian's maturity and correction. He did not have his eyes shut to the defective behavior of the Corinthians, but at the same time, he was honest to see the improvement in their behavior and in their actions. How good it is that he could say that the representatives brought to him that spiritual refreshment that he needed.

"Both to My Own Spirit and to Yours"

Observe that Paul said that these representatives refreshed "my own spirit." Man consists of spirit, soul, and body (1 Thess. 5:23). The spirit and soul make up the immaterial part of man, while the body represents the material part. God communicates with His Spirit with the immaterial part of man, the soul/spirit. We must, however, make a distinction between the spirit which only man has and the soul which is the animated part of all living creatures. Man's spirit is a gift given to him by God. Since Jesus Christ came to save sinners, and since man is the only creature that has a spirit, God communicates His spiritual life called eternal life to all who call upon Him. It is this spiritual life that fellow believers can cause to mature or to suffer loss. It can be refreshed or discouraged by fellow believers and others.

In dealing with the church of Corinth, Paul's spirit was depressed many times. In this instance, as the three representatives brought a letter to him while he was in Ephesus, their presence brought refreshment to the spirit of Paul. This is why he speaks of his own (*tó*, the neuter article; *emón*, the accusative singular neuter first person of the possessive pronoun *emós* [1699], mine, meaning my own) individual spirit.

Paul was interested not only in the refreshment of his own spirit, but also in the spirit of the Corinthians. He knew they needed much refreshment in view of the totally idolatrous environment in which they lived and the sin that beset them.

"Therefore Recognize Such Ones"

Paul adds a commandment concerning the Corinthian attitude toward the three men representing the church who brought the letter to him in Ephesus. He said, "Therefore recognize such ones."

The command "recognize" is the verb *epiginṓskete*, the second person plural present active imperative of *epiginṓskō* (1921), to experientially or personally know. It is derived from the preposition *epí* (1909), upon, indicating concentration, and *ginṓskō* (1097), to know experientially. The compound verb in the setting in which the Apostle Paul is using it means to recognize and to know who a person really is and what he has accomplished.

In this context, Paul is admonishing the Corinthians to recognize these men for what they had accomplished and for what they had known personally from experience.

The active voice indicates that it was the responsibility of the Corinthian believers to acknowledge all that the names of each one of the three delegates represented.

The present tense means that they were to do it all the time and not only occasionally, such as when they brought their letter to Paul, for that was an arduous journey.

The compound verb means to know experientially and fully. It was as if Paul was stressing the necessity of each of the Corinthian believers to become personally and fully knowledgeable of what these men had accomplished, not only for him but for all the Corinthian believers. By using the present imperative, Paul encourages them to continue to recognize and respect these Christian workers among them.

Paul mentions only the bringing of the letter from Corinth to Ephesus and possibly waiting for his answer to the Corinthian church. That alone was significant to both Paul and the church, and it should be an act that produced recognition that should not be forgotten.

The Apostle Paul does not want us to recognize only those who have served, but to recognize that we ourselves are also a unique people. In 2 Corinthians 13:5, he says, "Or do you not fully know [*epiginṓskete*, the second person plural present active indicative of *epiginṓskō*] your own selves, how that Jesus Christ is in you?" It is the duty of each one of us to examine himself to see whether he has this personal experience of Christ within him. We must not just assume that we belong to the family of God.

The knowledge that we have of others is only a partial knowledge. This is recognized by Paul in 1 Corinthians 13:9, "But we know in part." The verb here is *ginṓskomen* and it refers to the knowledge that is experientially possible for man to have. Paul is speaking of how he was recognized by the fellow Corinthians, but it was only a partial knowledge. He says in 2 Corinthians 1:14, "As also you have acknowledged us in part [*apó* {575}, from; *mérous*, the genitive of the singular neuter noun *méros* {3313}, part]." Since our knowledge of others is only partial, we do not know everything that is to be known concerning them, and naturally our estimation and appreciation of others is not exactly as it should be had we known in full all about them.

In our verse under examination, Paul indicates that we should recognize believers who have gone out of their way to do God's work and minister to His servants. We do not need to know everything about a person in order to recognize his character which a single act may have made manifest only partially.

LESSONS:

1. The spirit of the Apostle Paul was disturbed, and it needed rest and refreshment besides the refreshment that the Lord was always bringing to him.
2. We must recognize that in spite of the participation in the faith of Jesus Christ, we believers have the function of encouragement and consolation which will result in the recognition of others who are doing something for God.
3. We should give continuous recognition to those who are serving faithfully in ministry to others.

1 Cor. 16:19 | *Loving Remembrances*

The churches of Asia greet you. Aquila and Priscilla greet you much in the Lord together with the church in their house.

Paul has written in detail to the Corinthian church advising, admonishing, and encouraging them. We now come to the end of this letter in which he sends loving and encouraging greetings from himself and other believers to the members of the Corinthian church.

"The Churches of Asia Greet You"

Greetings are expressed by the Greek verb *aspázomai* (782), to embrace, salute, transitively spoken of those who meet or separate. In New Testament language it is equivalent to "peace be unto you" by those who meet (Luke 24:36 [TR]; John 20:19, 21, 26). Spoken of those who separate, it is equivalent to the expression "go in peace" (Mark 5:34; Luke 7:50; 8:48; Acts 15:33; 16:36). The noun is *aspasmós* (783), a salutation or greeting either orally or by letter (Matt. 23:7; Mark 12:38; Luke 1:29, 41, 44; 11:43; 20:46; 1 Cor. 16:21; Col. 4:18; 2 Thess. 3:17).

What did "embracing" (Acts 20:1; Heb. 11:13) include? In addition to words of greeting, it could include a kiss, an offering of the hand, or even falling on one's knees and kissing the other person's feet. These acts of affection could be expressed in a letter or in person. It indicates paying respect to someone. In the Septuagint of the Old Testament *aspázomai* is used in Exodus 18:7; Judges 18:15; Esther 5:2, plus several times in the Apocrypha.

We would understand more readily the importance and value of such greetings if we could easily comprehend the difficulty of communication at that time. As we see from these epistles, letters were hand-carried, and to deliver a letter and receive a reply may have taken weeks, if not months. The loving remembrance, then, of friends and fellow believers was a most important part of the communication. In the Epistles, it occurs forty-eight times. However, it is not found in Galatians, Ephesians, 2 Thessalonians, 1 Timothy, James, 2 Peter, 1 John or Jude. The Apostle Paul must have regarded the greeting as a very important expression of affection, for he uses it four times in verses 19 and 20. He used it to send greetings from a church as a whole or from individuals (Rom. 16:21ff.). The whole church undoubtedly wanted to be remembered (2 Cor. 13:13; Phil. 4:22). Besides, he sent a special greeting by the church of Ephesus and the churches of Asia to the church in Corinth (cf. Rom. 16:16).

The churches of which Paul is speaking in our verse under examination are identified by their location as the churches of Asia (1 Cor. 16:19; Col. 4:15; Phile. 2). The greeting was addressed to the church in Corinth. In Acts 8:1; 11:22, the church in Jerusalem was referred to. In Romans 16:1 the church at Cenchrea is mentioned. In 1 Thessalonians 1:1 and 2 Thessalonians 1:1, the church of Thessalonica is referred to. It is noteworthy to mention that the word "church" (*ekklēsía* [1577]) is not mentioned in Mark, Luke, John, 2 Timothy, Titus, 1 and 2 Peter, 1 and 2 John, or Jude.

Paul sends greetings from people to people. Never in the New Testament is the building in which a church meets called a "church." The people who are believers constitute the church. We have the church in Jerusalem (Acts 8:1; 11:22), Antioch (Acts 11:26; 13:1), Corinth (1 Cor. 1:2; 2 Cor. 1:1), Asia Minor (1 Cor. 16:19), Galatia (Gal. 1:2), Thessalonica (1 Thess. 1:1; 2 Thess. 1:1), Laodicea (Col. 4:16), and Cenchrea (Rom. 16:1). Also, we find "the churches of the nations" which means the churches of the Gentile Christians (Rom. 16:4), churches which meet in houses (Rom. 16:5; 1 Cor. 16:19; Phile. 2), the churches of Christ (Rom. 16:16), and the church of God at Corinth (1 Cor. 1:2).

In Jerusalem, individual believers were gathered at Pentecost from all over, including Asia (Acts 2:8–11). It is noteworthy that Paul does not say the **church** of Asia, but the **churches** (1 Cor. 16:19) of Asia, as if to indicate their independence and individuality.

Although individual churches are meant to be distinguished by the places in which groups of believers form a gathering together (*sunagōgḗ* [4864], synagogue), yet there is one church, the universal, which the Lord Jesus established. The first mention of the church is in Matthew 16:18 which the Lord Jesus called "My church": "And I say also unto you, that you are Peter, and upon this rock [your confession that I am the Christ, the Son of the living God] I will build My church [*ekklēsía*]; and the gates of hell shall not prevail against it." This universal church is also referred to in 1 Corinthians 12:28, Galatians 1:13, Ephesians 1:22; 3:10, and Hebrews 2:12; 12:23. It is also referred to as the church of God in 1 Corinthians 10:32; 11:22; 15:9 and 1 Timothy 3:15 as well as several other places.

The churches of Asia were the churches of Antioch and the seven churches of Asia Minor referred to in Revelation 2 and 3.

"Aquila and Priscilla Greet You Much in the Lord Together With the Church in Their House"

Soon after the Lord Jesus announced the establishment of His own universal church (Matt. 16:18), He said, "For where two or three are gathered together in My name, there am I in the midst of them" (Matt. 18:20). For a local church to be formed, it does not have to have a specified number of believers. It may be even two or three who, through their belief, demonstrate that they are leaving the world insofar as its spiritual influence is concerned, having been called out of it into an assembly of believers.

There were two individual believers, a couple whom Paul had met in Corinth by the names of Aquila and Priscilla (Acts 18:1–3, 18, 26; Rom. 16:3; 1 Cor. 16:19; 2 Tim. 4:19) who established a church in their home. Evidently this group met with the full approval of Paul. Aquila was a Jew whereas Priscilla was apparently a converted Roman. It seems they were people of means, and they maintained a house church at Ephesus and at Rome. When Paul went to Ephesus, Aquila and Priscilla went with him and remained there to minister while he visited Jerusalem. Thus, much of the initial work in Ephesus was done by Aquila and Priscilla. A little later we meet them in Rome, where, quite likely, they had been sent by Paul to prepare the way for his coming there. Aquila and Priscilla were very special to Paul, as Romans 16:3, 4 indicates. They later returned to Ephesus (2 Tim. 4:19). Since they were well–known to the Corinthians, Paul sends special greetings from them to the whole Corinthian church.

LESSONS:

1. We must distinguish between the universal church established by Jesus Christ (Matt. 16:18) and local churches known by the name of their location.

2. Although there were factions in Corinth and believers became known by the name of the leader they followed, Paul does not in any way speak of churches that bear the name of those individuals (1 Cor. 1:11–17).
3. There was an affinity and a relationship between one church and another church, and they were known by the region in which they were found, such as the churches of Asia, the churches of Galatia, and so on.
4. Each church had its own leaders.
5. Special greetings are extended to the Corinthian church from Aquila and Priscilla who were well-known to them and were beloved to Paul.
6. In addition to the church of Ephesus, this couple had established a church in their own home which later may have been incorporated into the church at Ephesus. Paul shows no objection to a church established in a home.
7. It would be well for each church to maintain fellowship with other churches at various locations in the interest of true Christian unity.

1 Cor. 16:20 | *Manifestation of Sanctified Love*

All the brethren greet you. Greet each other with a holy kiss.

This Epistle of Paul to the Corinthians has many chidings and corrections. Throughout his epistle, he intimates many things: they should not seek the wisdom of the world (1:20), but should boast in the Lord only (v. 31); they should be taught of the Holy Spirit (2:10); they should not be carnal (3:1–3); they should not seek physical prosperity but apostolic self-sacrifice (ch. 4); they should not tolerate fornication in their midst (ch. 5); they should not go to court for the sake of material benefits (6:1–11); they should realize that their body is the dwelling place of the Holy Spirit (6:18–20); they should take marriage seriously and not easily divorce (ch. 7); they should be careful how they live in an idolatrous society (8—10); their women should not shave their heads or leave them uncovered as did prostitutes who were looking for customers (11:1–16); they should not allow their love feasts to degenerate to a show of abundance (11:17–22); they should not take the Lord's Supper lightly and thus partake of it unworthily (11:23–34); they should not consider the body of Christ divided because of spiritual gifts, but they should remember that gifts come from God and should be used variably to accomplish His designed function and purpose (ch. 12); their whole life should be permeated by divine love (ch. 13); their speech should be in an understandable language that others can comprehend and not consider them mad (ch. 14); they should accept the resurrection of Christ as a fact of history which makes all the difference in the Christian faith (ch. 15); they should be concerned for others, although they might be far away (16:1–4); they should realize that although Paul is an apostle, he does not know the future and must have the right to make and change plans (16:5–12), and that they needed to be exhorted (16:13–18).

"All the Brethren Greet You"

After all these admonitions, we find Paul still considering them to be brothers, worthy to be greeted by fellow believers whom he also calls "brothers."

He calls the Corinthians "brothers" a total of thirty-eight times in his first epistle and twelve times in the second epistle. In spite of all their shortcomings, they are still brothers. Paul not only wrote about God's love, but he demonstrated that it was in his heart. It was expressed by him by the verb *aspázontai*, the third person plural present middle deponent indicative of *aspázomai* (782), to greet, salute, with which he begins this verse. Paul came to Ephesus after he left Corinth, having labored there a year and a half. In spite of the shortcomings of the Corinthians, he tried to instill love in the hearts of one church for another. This is why he says, "All the brethren greet you."

Paul wrote two authoritative epistles from Ephesus, almost at the same time. One was the first epistle to the Corinthians and the other to the Galatians. He closes this first epistle with greetings and love from the brethren of Ephesus to the brethren at Corinth. And in the epistle to the Galatians, he closes with the words, "brethren . . . amen." Paul does not use the words "brother" and "brothers" in the sense of belonging to the same earthly family or to the Jewish community, but to the family of Christ our Lord, thus differentiating them from those who do not belong to Him (cf. 1 Cor. 5:11; 6:5; 7:12; Gal. 6:10). In John 13:35, the Lord Jesus declares this divine love in the hearts of the disciples as a characteristic virtue when He said, "By this shall all men know that you are My disciples, if you have love one to another." Christians may be different one from another, but they must understand that there are diverse divine endowments which have all been given by God Himself (1 Cor. 4:7; 12:11). There is, however, one endowment which all Christians should have in common and which springs from faith in Christ. It is love (1 John 5:1). This divine love is not possessed in common by those who are not born again. The Lord Himself said, "A new [*kainḗn* {2537}, qualitatively new] commandment I give unto you, that you love one another [*allḗlous* {240}, one another but of the same kind, that is, believers]; as I have loved you, that you also love one another" (John 13:34). There is diversity in the Christian family, in the body of Christ, and in the function of each individual, but love and cooperation are to be manifest in each one so that there may be the accomplishment of God's work through the whole body of Christ. Members of the body of Christ must not fight one other, but cooperate with each other, no matter how different they are. Paul says in 1 Thessalonians 4:9 that to love one another is something that is taught of God: "But as touching brotherly love you need not that I write unto you: for you yourselves are taught of God to love one another." This divine love in the heart of the believer is a test of living or not living in God (1 John 3:14; 4:12).

Paul's greetings do not come from **some** of the Ephesian brethren, but from **all** of them. The word "all" is translated from *pántes*, the nominative plural masculine adjectival form of *pás* (3956), everyone. This *pántes* means all individuals, and "you" (*humás*) in the phrase "greet you" also means individuals. Not one individual was excluded from sending greetings of love to the brethren in Corinth. Paul did not in any way differentiate among the believers in Corinth, in spite of the fact that he knew of their divisions and the level of their commitment to Christ being different one from another. When we speak of our brethren in another place, do we distinguish some as being more worthy of love than others?

"Greet Each Other with a Holy Kiss"

The second sentence in this verse uses the word *aspázomai* on the occasion of Paul's letter being read to them, but it is the second person plural aorist middle imperative *aspásasthe*, meaning "this one time." The Corinthian church was certainly made up of a diverse group of people, but they all had the love of God in their hearts to some degree, and they considered themselves children of God, having been born of Him through Jesus Christ. All believers should be filled with the love of God, no matter where they are or how diverse their views are concerning nonessential things as long as they stand in the faith (v. 13) and have the blessed hope of the Lord's return.

The means whereby they should express their mutual love is designated by Paul as "with a holy kiss." The word *phílēma* (5370), kiss, comes from the verb *philéō* (5368), to love, have affection for, to have the same interests as another. A kiss is the expression of human love, whereas *agápē* (26) is the divine love implanted in the human heart by God Himself as a result of believing in His Son, the Lord Jesus Christ. The father of the prodigal son kissed him when he returned home. That meant that he accepted him and reconciled himself to him (Luke 15:20). So a kiss is a sign of acceptance and reconciliation. It is also a sign of gratitude. The Ephesian elders kissed Paul in gratitude for what he meant to them (Acts 20:37). But why did Judas kiss the Lord Jesus when he betrayed Him (Mark 14:44,

45)? It was a kiss of hypocrisy. The greatest characteristic of love can be the greatest indication of hypocrisy, too.

A kiss is usually touching the lips to another's lips, cheeks, shoulder, hands, or feet, as a gesture of friendship. When it came to kissing Jesus, however, except in the case of Judas, it was an act of gratitude and respect. The woman, for instance, who kissed Jesus in appreciation for the forgiveness of her sins kissed Him on His feet, not on the mouth nor on the face (Luke 7:38). This was the kiss that is often expressed as *proskunéō* (4352). It literally means to kiss like a dog licking his master's feet, to prostrate one's self in homage, respect or worship.

As love takes the form of lust (*epithumía* [1939]), so the word "kiss" is used most commonly among people for the expression of fleshly desire. It is related to *hēdonḗ* (2237), hedonism or pleasure or passion (*páthos* [3806], inordinate desire). These are the kisses that worldly people so often engage in, and they are related to the verb *eráō*, to love in a lustful way. This verb is not found at all in the New Testament.

To differentiate lustful kisses from sanctified kisses, Paul used the word *hágios* (40), sanctified, saintly. The kissing of each other meant that the believers belonged to each other not lustfully, but together in the family of God, to Jesus Christ. It showed their affection for Him and for each other, for they are commanded to externalize that love. We can do this in many ways, but when we do it with a kiss, let us make sure that it remains a holy kiss, not a sensual one.

LESSONS:

1. Paul did not speak to the Ephesians concerning the weaknesses of the Corinthians, although there were many. Thus brotherly love was encouraged in the hearts of the Ephesians for the Corinthians, and Paul could truthfully say, "They all send greetings to you."

2. The letter of Paul purposed to unify the Corinthians and to show them that the main characteristic of faith is the divine love in their hearts which was to be expressed through a holy kiss.
3. Christians must guard themselves and never allow a holy kiss of love to become a kiss of lust.
5. It would be well for the brethren today to be able to encourage one another in a holy embrace as a sign of the unity that we have in Christ.

1 Cor. 16:21 — *Paul Assures His Letter's Authenticity*

The greeting is in my own hand, Paul's.

The Apostle Paul did not necessarily write with his own hand the epistles he addressed to different churches. In Romans 16:22, we read, "I, Tertius, who wrote this epistle, salute you in the Lord."

"The Greeting Is in My Own Hand, Paul's"

We do not know who acted as Paul's secretary in this instance or whom Paul used to write the First Epistle to the Corinthians. However, he added his own signature to the letter to prove that it was authentic. He closes his letter in 2 Thessalonians exactly the same way that he closes this letter to the Corinthians. On the other hand, in his letter to the Galatians, he informs them that he, himself, wrote the epistle either in its entirety or partly (Gal. 6:11). The epistle to Philemon Paul wrote with his own hand in its entirety.

The genitive *Paulou* (Paul's) goes with the nominative "the greeting" (*ho aspasmós* [783], the greeting), meaning "the greeting of Paul." The verb to be understood is *esti*, the third person singular present indicative of *eimí* (1510), to be. *Tē̃ emē̃ cheirí* should be translated as "is in my own hand," the possessive pronoun *emē̃* and the noun *cheirí* being in the dative. This is as if to say, as when anyone signs a letter now, that his very signature attests to the genuineness of the content of the letter. In addition, Paul affixes his signature at the beginning of every letter that he wrote, stating that he is the author of it. So we have the signature of the author at the beginning of the letter and the statement at the end, affirming that all that is said in the letter is from him.

LESSONS:

1. Paul signs this letter with his own name to indicate to the Corinthians that he is the author of it.
2. At that time, as even today, spurious letters were sent out as we see in 2 Thessalonians 2:2 as if they were from Paul but really were not.
3. Note that 2 Thessalonians 2:2 says, "That you be not soon shaken in mind, or be troubled, neither by spirit, nor by word, **nor by letter as from us**, as that the day of Christ is at hand." Paul did not want the Corinthian letter to lack authenticity.
4. We would do well to be as specific and accurate in all we write as Paul was.

1 Cor. 16:22 | *Unbelief Has Certain, Prophetic Consequences*

If anyone does not befriend the Lord Jesus Christ, let him be reserved unto judgment. Our Lord comes.

In the body of his letter to the Corinthians, Paul discussed many problems of the Christian life. He wanted to add a postscript with his own hand to all that he had said to them. He must have been faced with a dilemma as to what to say in conclusion. As is his custom, he proceeds to say it with the supposition of subjective hypothesis, not of reality.

The teaching of the Apostle Paul was that Jesus Christ came into a sinful world to die to redeem men. This is the gospel that Paul personally delivered to the Corinthians (1 Cor. 15:3, 4), and this is the reason why God, who is Spirit, became man, without sin, so that He could shed His innocent blood to save sinners from their sin (Heb. 4:15; 7:27; 9:12; 10:10).

God desired that all men should repent and believe and thus be saved. Paul also desired that as many as possible might be saved through the example of his life and his preaching (1 Cor. 9:19). Both Christ and His elect apostle knew, nevertheless, that salvation could not be imposed upon mankind if they were to retain their freedom of will. And so in order that salvation might become a reality in the lives of men, they had to believe to receive the free gift of eternal life (John 3:16). The Lord knew, however, as did also Paul, that not all men would believe and thus they would not be saved (1 John 2:2; Titus 2:11; 1 Tim. 2:4, 6; 2 Pet. 3:9). Paul fully understood that if people were going to perish, it was not due to the will of God, but to the will of man through refusing to repent and accept God's gift of eternal life. Man was given the privilege of choice, but he was not given the privilege of choosing the consequences of his choice.

"If Anyone Does Not"

The consequence of man's choice was eternally and irrevocably set by God Himself. Nevertheless, God must not receive the blame for man's unbelief, for God prepared hell for the devil and his angels (Matt. 25:41), and man only goes there by his choice. Therefore, the suppositional "if" in this verse is *ei* (1487), the subjective "if" that is entirely hypothetical. It is not *eán* (1437) which is the supposition of reality and experience. Thus Paul wanted to close his epistle by telling the Corinthians that the choice by some not to love the Lord Jesus Christ and become His friend is indeed theirs, but he wanted them at the same time to realize what will come at the end of the road when they meet their Maker.

The next word is translated "anyone" (*tis* [5100], the indefinite pronoun meaning "someone"). This pinpoints the man who has made a decision not to believe on Christ, but it indicates that it makes no difference who that person is. It could be anyone, he could have any amount of money, he could have any amount of fame and even belong to the Hall of Fame that humans have erected. It is man's privilege to believe or not to believe in Christ, but he must suffer the consequences of not believing if he rejects the gospel, and he will start enjoying the benefits of believing here and now if he does believe, and there will be no end to them.

The next word is the absolute "not" (*ou* [3756]). There are no half-believers. Faith in Jesus Christ gives the believer the basic privilege of entering the kingdom of God. If that decision is made in the Holy Spirit, it is final and irrevocable (John 3:16–18; 10:28).

"Befriend the Lord Jesus Christ"

Paul now uses a verb in this letter that he only uses here in 1 Corinthians 16:22. Being rendered "love" by the translators (KJV) would lead the reader to believe that Paul uses the verb *agapáō* (25), to love with the divinely implanted love, or the noun *agápē* (26), that divine love with which God loved man and which He miraculously implants in his heart when he believes. It is this kind of love that Paul speaks about so profusely in his Corinthian and other epistles. However, this is the only verse where Paul uses the verb *philéō* (5368), to befriend. The verb *philéō* comes from *phílos* (5384), friend, and a friend is a person who shares the same interests as someone else and demonstrates that friendship in his attachment to that person. The reader is advised to read the discussion under the verb *philéō* in *The Complete Word Study Dictionary: New Testament.* To be a friend of the Lord Jesus Christ involves adopting His interests and making them become one's own. The person who neglects to do this rejects Christ. He does not respond to His love for salvation, nor does he follow after the Lord.

The verb *philéō* is in the present indicative which demonstrates that Paul is speaking about a person who does not want to have anything to do with Christ at any time. This is a person who is either an enemy of Christ or totally indifferent to Christ.

Can any human being in his own power befriend the Lord Jesus Christ? This is inherently impossible because God is holy and man is a sinner from the day of the fall of Adam. He is estranged from God and has made himself an enemy of God

(Rom. 5:10). In fact, the word *echthrós* (2190), enemy, is the opposite of *phílos*, friend, to which the verb *philéō*, to befriend, is related. Man in his fallen condition, being an enemy of God, naturally is not going to befriend Jesus Christ. He must first be reconciled to God (2 Cor. 5:18–21). The Lord Jesus not only became man, but He died to make us God's friends (Rom. 5:8). In response to His undeserved love for us we believe in Him and are transformed into new creatures (2 Cor. 5:17). Then we begin to love God and desire His companionship. This is the *agápē* love of God.

In our unregenerated state, we cannot befriend Jesus Christ for He is perfectly holy while we are still sinners. However, He is called "the friend of publicans and sinners" (Matt. 11:19; Luke 7:34). How can this be then? Jesus sought to win sinners to Himself and cause them to experience His love. He never made friends of sinners by making their interests His interests, for He has never tasted sin (Heb. 4:15). The Lord Jesus said, "You are my friends, if you do whatever I command you. Henceforth I call you not servants; for the servant knows not what his lord does: but I have called you friends; for all things that I have heard of my Father I have made known unto you" (John 15:14, 15). He called Lazarus His friend because he was a saved man (John 11:11). Abraham was called a friend of God because he was ready to do what God did in sacrificing His son (James 2:21–23).

The Lord Jesus is designated in 1 Corinthians 16:22 as "the Lord [*Kúrios* {2962}] Jesus Christ." This is His full name. First of all, He is the Lord, which is a name ascribed to God the Father. God is called *Kúrios* in the New Testament and in Old Testament quotations or allusions (Mark 1:3; 12:11, etc.). God the Father is the Jehovah of the Old Testament, but He is a separate Person from the Lord Jesus Christ, the Son who has always been with the Father (John 1:1, 18) and the Second Person of the Triune God.

Kúrios is also used for the historical Jesus (cf. Acts 11:16; 20:35; 1 Cor. 9:5; 1 Thess. 4:15; Heb. 2:3). The very fact that Paul uses the word "Lord" prior to the historical name of Jesus is a demonstration, indeed, that Jesus was the Lord, and He is the only One who walked upon this earth who is Lord, who was Lord, and always will be Lord (1 Cor. 8:6; Heb. 13:8).

The third name ascribed to the historical Jesus is "Christ" (*Christós* [5547]) meaning the Messiah, the Anointed of the Father.

Actually, for man not to befriend such an almighty God who humbled Himself to the point of dying for us (Phil. 2:6–8) is suicidal (Matt. 21:44; Luke 20:18). If anyone has an opportunity to become the friend of the Almighty, and refuses to do it on His terms, he is certainly not acting in his own best interests (Rev. 1:8; 4:8; 11:17; 15:3; 16:7, 14; 19:6, 15; 21:22).

"Let Him Be Reserved Unto Judgment"

Our verse says that a person who has the opportunity of becoming a friend of the almighty God and refuses to do so places himself in direct line of judgment to come.

Is the Apostle Paul pronouncing a curse upon such a man or is the curse a consequence of his choice?

First, to come to an understanding, we must examine the verb *ḗtō* (2277), let him be, which is the third person singular present imperative of *eimí* (1510), to be. Is this a statement of fact that is inevitable, or is it a wish? Does the Apostle Paul wish a curse to come upon the one who has not chosen to befriend the Lord Jesus Christ? Of course that could not be! Nor does the Lord Jesus, who predicts the punishment which will come upon the unbeliever. Rather, He declares the punishment that will come with certainty and inevitability so that it may be avoided, but He does not make the punishment His wish. The heart of God and those who proclaim His message is expressed in 2 Peter 3:9: "but is longsuffering to usward, not willing [*boulómenos*, the nominative singular masculine present middle deponent participle of *boúlomai* {1014}, to desire, wish, expressing an inner predisposition] that any should perish, but that all should come to repentance." This is the heart of God and the heart of the Apostle Paul who wanted to win as many as possible to Christ (1 Cor. 9:19) and should be the heart of every believer as well. God does not prepare people for eternal damnation, but does warn of eternal damnation in the absence of repentance and faith. A verse that must be properly understood is Romans 9:22: "What if God, willing to show His wrath, and to make His power known, endured with much longsuffering the vessels of wrath fitted to destruction?" In Greek grammar, we have three voices—the active, the middle, and the passive. In English, we have only two, the active and the passive. The verb "fit them" (*katērtisména* [2675]) can be either a passive or a middle participle. If it is taken as passive, it presupposes God as being the One who fits unbelievers to destruction. If taken in the middle voice, it means that people personally fit themselves to destruction by not repenting and believing. We must not forget that unbelief and lack of repentance have built in them the judgment that pertains to them. John 3:17, 18 states God's intent very clearly: "For God sent not [*ou*, the absolute negative] His Son into the world to condemn the world; but that the world through Him might be saved. He who believes on Him is not [*ou*] condemned: but he who believes not [*mḗ* {3361}, the relative negative] is condemned already, because he has not believed in the name of the only-begotten Son of God."

The word which is often translated "accursed" is the noun *anáthema* which has also become the English word "anathema." This is an imprecation which has come to mean an accursed person or thing. It comes from the verb *anatíthēmi* (394), to separate, lay up. *Anáthēma* was a consecrated gift hung up or laid up in the temple (Luke 21:5). *Anathémata* (331) were gifts dedicated to God's glory, such as the shield, chaplets, golden chains, and candlesticks. Such offerings were and still are common in heathen temples and in Greek Orthodox and Catholic churches. The noun then came to mean that which is laid up for the judgment of God. The verb *anathematízō* (332) came to mean to bind by a curse (Acts 23:12, 14, 21) or simply to curse (Mark 14:71). To "suffer a curse" was to be laid up for the sure judgment of God.

In 1 Corinthians 16:22, it means that he who has not made a friend of the Lord Jesus Christ is laid up for God's judgment and, therefore, is accursed. This however, does not mean that God has willfully cursed him, but that he will surely one day reap the consequence of his choice not to be a friend of the Lord Jesus Christ, having had the opportunity to repent and believe on Him and thereby accept His love (*agápē*).

This word also occurs in 1 Corinthians 12:3 as a preamble to Paul's discussion on spiritual gifts where he says, "Wherefore I give you to understand, that no man speaking by the Spirit of God calls Jesus accursed [*anáthema*]: and that no man can say that Jesus is the Lord, but by the Holy Ghost." A person cannot acknowledge that Jesus is the Lord without the Holy Spirit. No one is a friend of the Lord Jesus Christ who does not submit himself to the convicting power of the Holy Spirit.

"Our Lord Comes"

There is yet another word which concludes this verse and which is found only here. It is an Aramaic word, *marán athá* (3134), the Lord has come, or, according to an Ethiopic version, "at the coming of the Lord." This word was adopted by the early church in conjunction with the celebration of the Lord's Supper.

In the discussion about the Lord's Supper in 1 Corinthians 11:23–26, Paul definitely tells us that this is a celebration to commemorate the death of the Lord Jesus, and it is to be clearly declared until He comes. In our exegesis of 1 Corinthians 11:26, we pointed out that the verb pinpoints the coming of the Lord although the exact time is unknown. The verb is *élthē,* the third person singular second aorist active subjunctive of *érchomai* (2064), to come. This is different from other forms of the verb which describe His coming: (1) the participle meaning the "coming One" (Matt. 3:11; 11:3; 21:9; 23:39; 24:30; Mark 11:9; 13:26; Luke 7:19, 20; 13:35; 19:38; 21:27; John 1:15, 27; 3:31; 6:14, 35; 11:27; 12:13; 2 Cor. 11:4; Heb. 10:37; Rev. 1:4, 8; 4:8); (2) the first person present indicative meaning, "I am coming" (John 14:3, 18, 28; 21:22, 23; Rev. 2:5, 16; 3:11; 16:15; 22:7, 12, 20); or (3) the third person present indicative meaning "He is coming" (Matt. 21:5; 24:42–44; 25:19; Mark 1:7; Luke 12:39, 40; John 1:30; 12:15; 1 Thess. 5:2; Rev. 1:7).

When Jesus instituted the Lord's Supper in Matthew 26:26–30, in verse 29 he related to His coming back to establish the actual kingdom of His Father (cf. Mark 14:22–25, especially v. 25). In 1 Corinthians 11:26, Paul was very explicit that the Lord's Supper will be celebrated until the Lord realizes His Second Coming. "Till" is *hoú*, the genitive singular masculine of the relative pronoun *hós* (3739) with *chrónou* (5550), time, implied. In Greek *hoú* is followed by the conjunction *án* (302), if, since, indicating that the event described will certainly happen at any time. *Élthē*, the third person singular second aorist active subjunctive of *érchomai* (2064), to come, must be in the subjunctive because of the conjunction *án*. This conjunction *án* basically means "if" of reality which, because of the certainty of the event, should be translated "when." Thus we have "when such time as He will come" or "should come." Paul taught that this event is certain; it is pinpointed, and he refers only to the coming of the Lord for His saints who have died and who will be resurrected and receive their new bodies (1 Thess. 4:15, 16), and the living saints who will be changed (1 Cor. 15:51) to fit the new environment into which they will be ushered.

This is a time when believers are going to receive their rewards (Luke 14:14; 2 Cor. 5:10), and the time of the tribulation for the unbelievers will be introduced as elaborated upon in the Book of Revelation, chapters 6—19. This is the day of *anáthema,* of the curse that unbelievers brought upon themselves as a consequence of their unbelief and not having become friends of Christ. It is the day of judgment which has already begun concurrently with their unbelief (John 3:18) and will reach its ultimate fulfillment when the Lord comes for His saints. Simultaneously, it will be the Day of the Lord or the Day of Judgment for unbelievers as it is the Day of Christ for the believers. No wonder the early church celebrated the Lord's Supper by closing with the word *marán athá*, the Lord come or the Lord has come, using the word in anticipation of His certain fulfillment called the prophetic future.

LESSONS:

1. It is indeed folly to realize who the Lord Jesus Christ is and not respond to His love and become His friend, sharing His interest in anticipation of the fulfillment of His prophecies concerning His coming.
2. The word translated "befriend" in this verse is not the oft-repeated *agapáō* nor the noun *agápē* spoken so often by Paul (1 Cor. 13), but it is the verb *philéō* which means to befriend, related to the word *philía*, friendship.
3. The two words, *agapáō* and *philéō* are best understood when one carefully analyzes the conversation that the risen Christ had with the Apostle Peter in John 21:15–19. Peter confessed that though he fell short of the supreme and sacrificial love of Christ (*agapáō* which is a response to His love), he was His real friend (*philéo*) and wanted to make the interests of Christ his own interests. Since that was the case, the Lord entrusted Peter with the shepherding of His flock.

4. In this verse, the Lord Jesus is presented in His full title to indicate what a great Friend He is and to indicate the folly of refusing to make Him one's own personal Friend.
5. The curse here ought not to be understood as the desire of the Lord or Paul to anathematize or curse those who do not love Him. It rather indicates that they are simply reaping the consequence of their own choice by not choosing to become friends of Christ.
6. The judgment that is to come upon unbelievers is definitely connected with the Lord's coming which the word *marán athá* says, "The Lord come." It is a day of great tribulation for the unbeliever (Rev. 6–19), but of great blessing and expectation for the Christian (1 Thess. 4:13–18).

1 Cor. 16:23 | The Inexhaustible Reservoir of Grace

The grace of the Lord Jesus Christ be with you.

Verse 22 spoke of the judgment which will come upon man as a result of the consequence of his own sin, his refusal to become a friend of God while he had the opportunity. Jesus Christ became a man who evidenced that He was indeed God in the flesh and that He was the designated Messiah. Now, in this verse, Paul wants to stress the benevolence of God through Christ, and thus speaks of the grace of the Lord Jesus Christ.

"The Grace of the Lord Jesus Christ"

The Apostle Paul closes this first letter to the Corinthians with the word "grace" (*cháris* [5485], grace, favor). The favor of God brings a miracle into the life of an individual when accepted in faith. It transforms that person and causes him to love and to seek after the righteousness of God. Grace is initially regeneration, the work of the Holy Spirit in which spiritual life is imparted to man and by which his nature is brought under the dominion of righteousness. I quote from page 1,469 of my *Complete Word Study Dictionary: New Testament*:

> Grace (*cháris*) is initially regeneration, the work of the Holy Spirit in which spiritual life is given to man and by which his nature is brought under the dominion of righteousness. The maintenance of this condition

> requires an unbroken and immense supply of grace. Grace remains constant in, and basic to, a believer's fight without against the devil and his struggle within against sin. Renewal is stimulated and impelled by God's illuminating and strengthening of the soul, and will continue and increase so long as the soul perseveres. God's grace insures that those who have been truly regenerated will persevere until the end of life.

This regenerating and changing power of God in the human heart is made possible only through Christ, who again in this verse is called by His full name, "The Lord Jesus Christ." His omnipotence is emphasized by the word "Lord." His incarnation, humanity, and its uniqueness of having no sin (Heb. 4:15) is emphasized through the word "Jesus" which is the human name of that historic Personality that was the Word become flesh (John 1:1, 14). But He was not like any other human being born into the world—He was the eternal Christ who has always been in the bosom of the Father (John 1:18).

The whole revelation of Scripture closes with this benediction which believers, called "saints," have received and through which their lives have been changed. Revelation 22:21 reads, "The grace of our Lord Jesus Christ with you all. Amen" (TR).

God's Grace Is Available to All

We find this benediction at the end of 1 Corinthians because Paul wanted to stress that the grace of God is available to all living human beings, to be appropriated by faith alone. Notice that immediately after speaking of the judgment of God, Paul speaks of the grace of God. The Corinthian church was a worldly church into which much sin had crept. Paul spoke of the judgment of God as constituting part of the truth which came as a result of Jesus Christ. John speaks of grace before he speaks of truth (John 1:17). Grace, the changing power of God, is presented before the awful truth of the judgment of God. But Paul found it necessary in verse 22 to present the judgment of God, not because he was vindictive, but because this is the true consequence of man's choice. Then he said that the grace of the Lord Jesus Christ is available as long as man has life, because as Hebrews 9:27 says, "And as it is appointed unto men once to die, but after this the judgment." Grace is available as long as one lives, but not after death. Only a living person has the choice of making the Lord Jesus Christ the best Friend that anyone can have, and it is advantageous in life and after death. Because of this grace, Paul could say, "For to me to live is Christ, and to die *is* gain" (Phil. 1:21).

In the beginning of his letter to the Corinthians, the Apostle Paul stressed that the grace of God was given to them in Christ Jesus (1 Cor. 1:4). It is through this grace that the Corinthians who believed were enriched (v. 5). It is through this grace that they became God-sufficient (v. 7). And it is through this grace that they became a people full of expectation of something better to come.

However, there is one thing that Paul wants to stress in closing this letter to the Corinthians, and that is that the grace of God through Jesus Christ is an inexhaustible reservoir of power in the believer's life. The Apostle Paul, at the beginning of each of his epistles, wishes grace and peace to the recipients (Rom. 1:7; 1 Cor. 1:3; 2 Cor. 1:2; Gal. 1:3; Eph. 1:2; Phil. 1:2; Col. 1:2; 1 Thess. 1:1; 2 Thess. 1:2; 1 Tim. 1:2; 2 Tim. 1:2; Titus 1:4; Phile. 3). The typical opening wish is, Grace be unto you and peace from God our Father and the Lord Jesus Christ.

Without grace there can be no peace, for the two co-exist and interact in the human heart. They both come from God the Father and the Lord Jesus Christ. God the Father and God the Son participate in the dispensing of the grace and the peace that man needs. The one constitutes the source of salvation, and the other is the result of salvation.

Grace stands in antithesis to the law (Rom. 6:14). While formerly the blessings of God were secured by obedience to the law, today in the dispensation of the New Testament, they are obtained by grace.

Grace is also the antithesis of works because it is not something that a person earns, but it is something that is freely given by God (Rom. 4:4). It is not something good which can be bought by favors to God, but it is His own endowment which a believer undeservedly receives by faith (Gal. 3:6; Rom. 11:6). It is the free gift of God in Jesus Christ (Rom. 5:15), something that God gives because of Jesus Christ's sacrifice on the cross of Calvary and which can be received only by faith (Eph. 2:8).

What the Lord Jesus Christ can do for man, grace can do, for He is grace personified. We are called by grace (Gal. 1:15); we are justified by grace (Rom. 3:24); we are sanctified by grace (Rom. 6:14); through grace we obtain eternal comfort and good hope (2 Thess. 2:16), and grace makes us free and strong (1 Cor. 9:1, 19; 2 Tim. 2:1).

As Paul opens his epistles with grace, he closes them in the same way, in spite of all the chastisements that he pronounces in his epistles (Rom. 16:20–24; 1 Cor. 16:23; 2 Cor. 13:14; Gal. 6:18; Eph. 6:24; Phil. 4:23; Col. 4:18; 1 Thess. 5:28; 2 Thess. 3:18; 1 Tim. 6:21; 2 Tim. 4:22; Titus 3:15; Phile. 25).

The believer is immersed in grace initially, and once he has experienced this divine visitation, he will conclude his life with grace; he will experience it all in between, and he will be carried by grace into eternity.

In all the introductions of Paul in regard to the grace of God, he says that it is "from" (*apo* [575]). This marks the origin or source which is God the Father and the Lord Jesus Christ. By receiving the grace of God, a believer receives that which characterizes deity. When he was originally created, man was in the image of God and did not need to repent. The grace of God, which can be equated to the Person of the Lord Jesus Christ becoming the mediator between God the Father and sinful man, was necessitated because of man's sin. At the receiving of the Savior, the grace of God indwells the human heart and changes it (Rom. 8:10). When man believes, he receives the life that sin caused him to miss, that is, eternal life. Upon receiving the grace of God, when man receives Christ as his Lord and Savior, he does not exhaust that which is to be had of and in Christ. Christ continues to be an independent entity available for salvation and help to all humans.

"*Be* with You"

The word that means "participation in Christ" is the verb *metéchō* (3348), to partake, participate, to have in fellowship with, derived from *metá* (3326), with, and *échō* (2192), to have. To partake is to have together with others. The person who thus has something together with others is called *métochos* (3353), partaker. In the same way that we are partakers of Christ (Heb. 3:14), we are also partakers of grace (1 Cor. 10:30). We become by the grace of God what we are in Christ. In 1 Corinthians 15:10, Paul said, "By the grace of God I am what I am." But Christ and the grace of God are available as separate entities to help us in our infirmities. This is why in the closing greeting that Paul has for each church, his prayer is that believers not only have the grace of God in them, but with (*metá*) them (Rom 16:24; 1 Cor. 16:23; 2 Cor. 13:14; Gal. 6:18; Eph. 6:24; Phil. 4:23; Col. 4:18; 1 Thess. 5:28; 2 Thess. 3:18; 1 Tim. 6:21; 2 Tim. 4:22; Titus 3:15; Phile. 25). We can look at this as an independent, external entity available to the Christian, a reservoir for filling any gap within. This inexhaustible reservoir of grace is available as an independent Personality to be with believers as a source of strength and enablement.

LESSONS:

1. The Christian life begins with the initial input of grace through Jesus Christ, and it ends with whatever infilling of grace is necessary throughout the whole course of the Christian life.
2. The believer is not only meant to receive grace (1 Cor. 1:4–8) that is available in and through Jesus Christ for the changing of his own life so that every part of his being becomes gracious, but he is supposed to dispense that grace to others. As one receives freely, he ought to give freely (Matt. 10:8).
3. What the believer gives to others of the grace of God will not diminish his own reservoir, because God's reservoir of grace is inexhaustible and always available for the believer to draw upon. This is what is meant in John 1:16, "And of His fullness have all we received, and grace for [*antí* {473}, instead of, in lieu of, in substitution of] grace."
4. This grace ought to be distinguished as the Lord Jesus Christ and, therefore, different from any other gracious act of a fellow human being. Jesus Christ is God's saving and sustaining grace.
5. The world seeks peace through modern methods, but there can be no peace apart from the initial infusion of grace in one's soul and the continuous infilling as one faces the experiences and trials of life.
6. Christians who lack peace need to examine their position in Christ and their fellowship with Him.

1 Cor. 16:24 | Corrected, but Loved

My love be with you all in Christ Jesus. Amen.

In verse 23, Paul emphasized the grace of the Lord Jesus Christ. The word *cháris* (5485) is related to *chaírō* (5463), to rejoice, and *chará* (5479), joy, delight, the result of the activity of the grace of God in man. Without the forgiveness that the grace of God in Jesus Christ brings, there can be no joy of salvation. But this grace of God in Jesus Christ is the result of the intrinsic characteristic of God which is love. In 1 John 4:8, 16, the essence of God is love. Love is not blind. It is a twin sister of truth (2 John 3). God looked upon man who had fallen from the perfect state in which He made him originally. But God loved the world, not because the world was lovable, but because God in His mercy perceived man's great need.

Actually, the word *agapáō* (25), to love, is not the same as the verb *philéō* (5368), to befriend. The need of man is to be reconciled to God, whose enemy he became as a result of sin. In order to accomplish this miracle, it required sacrifice on the part of God, for without the shedding of blood, there could be no forgiveness, no release, from the enslaving power of sin (Heb. 9:22). But the blood shed, which could avail for the forgiveness of man's sin, had to be by a person without sin (Heb. 4:15). The only Person with that qualification was Jesus Christ who became man and was born of the Virgin Mary (John 1:14; Heb. 2:14; Matt. 1:18–25; Luke 1:26–37).

"My Love"

Paul stood in awe of such love of God. In 1 Corinthians 13:4, 8, 13 He describes it as **the** love because of its uniqueness. He appropriated that love and made it his own, so in closing 1 Corinthians, he could say, "My love." Paul had fought God's love with all his power, but he finally succumbed to it when the risen Christ appeared to him on the Damascus Road. How wonderful it is to say that **the** love has become **my** love.

In writing to the Corinthians in 1 Corinthians 13:6, Paul says that this love rejoices in the truth. The verb used in that verse is *sugchaírei*, the second person singular present active indicative of *sugchaírō* (4796), to rejoice together, and it is derived from the preposition *sún* (4862), together, and *chaírō*, to rejoice. It should be translated "love rejoices together with truth."

In 1 Corinthians, Paul was truthful to speak of people and situations as they were and not to cover them up. He spoke the truth because Jesus Christ who was sent by God into the world came "full of grace and truth" (John 1:14). He did not come to hide the truth that man was sinful and needed the transforming grace of God. Paul came to the Corinthians with the same attitude. He spoke the truth because he was not afraid of it since grace was available to heal all that was wrong with man. There is no wrong that grace cannot redeem. This is what James 5:20 has as the closing statement of his epistle: "He which converts a sinner from the error of his way shall save a soul from death, and shall cover a multitude of sins."

The verb *kalúpsei*, shall cover, the third person singular future active indicative of *kalúptō* (2572), has been misunderstood as meaning to hide. The meaning of this, however, has been caught by the translators of the Living Bible and Today's

English Version as "bring about the forgiveness of his many sins." This was Paul's desire in his first letter to the Corinthians. He saw their many sins, but they were sins of believers that needed correcting and which found their correction through the Apostle Paul. He thus could speak of "my love" as a truly corrective love that the Corinthians needed. And as his Master sacrificed His own life in order that this love might be expressed in grace, so Paul did everything that he could to show his spirit of sacrifice among the Corinthians.

How Great Is Our Love?

It is interesting to point out that our verse under study is the only place in the New Testament that the expression "my love" is found besides John 15:9, 10 when Jesus used these words. No other apostle spoke of his love. We refer the reader to our exegesis of 1 Corinthians 9:6 in which Paul says, "Or I only and Barnabas." Can any of us speak of our love (*agápē*) like the Apostle Paul did? And could we mean that our love was bathed in sacrifices for Christ who was willing to lay down His life for sinners and considered it all joy in looking at the cross and enduring it, despising its shame (Heb. 12:2)? Paul was indeed sincere when he wrote in Philippians 3:8, "Yes doubtless, I count all things *but* loss for the excellency of the knowledge of Christ Jesus my Lord: for whom I have suffered the loss of all things, and do count them but dung, that I may win Christ." Has any of us truly done that? If we have not, then we do not have the right to speak of our love for God, but only of His love for us. The Apostle John was the disciple of love, but he never spoke of his love for the Lord, but rather of the Lord's love for him (John 13:23; 19:26; 20:2; 21:7, 20). Such a saint as the Apostle John could never bring himself to speak of his love for Christ, for he was too humble. While it is perfectly proper and, in fact, desirable, for us to express our love to God in our private prayers, it somehow evidences pride when we tell others how much we love the Lord.

"Be with You All"

The preposition that Paul uses here to express his love for the Corinthians is *metá* (3326), with, implying accompaniment. He was sure that there were some who would not accept his love as genuine concern for the redemptive correction that he tried to bring about. We must realize that our love, no matter how sincere and truthful it is, cannot be forced upon others. Its acceptance is a work of grace in itself. However, this does not mean that it should not be exercised by those of us who have appropriated the love of God as our guideline.

Notice the next two words, "you all." In Greek it is *pántōn*, the genitive plural masculine adjectival form of *pás* (3956), all, and *humṓn* (5216), you, the genitive plural of the second person personal pronoun *sú* (4771). Paul was writing to everyone, to those who agreed with him and those who disagreed, especially in the exercise of the spiritual gifts that he had discussed with the Corinthians as with no one else (12—14).

In Corinth there was a "Paul party." Paul did not side with that party and say, I thank the Lord that I have some followers in Corinth who agree with me, but he said, "My love be with all of you." There were some who actively opposed him. Paul wanted to persuade the Corinthians that the only qualification for this particular love was that they be in Christ Jesus. We remind our readers that Paul used three chapters of this epistle, namely chapters 8, 9, and 10, to explain his position concerning the *adiáphora* (n.f.), the indifferent things or the nonessentials in which believers could exercise Christian freedom. Undoubtedly, there were many who disagreed with him, but nevertheless, he included them among all who were in Christ Jesus. The lives of all Christians are not uniform. The choices of some are not the choices of others. Not all sacrifice equally for the Lord. First John 5:1 says, "Whosoever believes that Jesus is the Christ is born of God: and everyone that loves Him that begat loves him also that is begotten of Him."

"In Christ Jesus. Amen"

The final expression that Paul uses is "in Christ Jesus," not "Jesus Christ." This expression stressed the deity of Christ first and then His humanity. The expression is also used after Acts 19:4, and the reason for stressing it in this verse is that both grace and love are divine characteristics which the new birth demonstrates in man.

As Paul closes his second epistle to the Corinthians, he refers to both grace and love as **the** grace and **the** love. "The grace of the Lord Jesus Christ, and the love of God, and the communion of the Holy Ghost, *be* with you all. Amen" (2 Cor. 13:14). The emphasis here is on the Trinity and on the specific function of each Person of the Trinity in the work of salvation. The grace is of the Lord Jesus Christ. The love is the love of the Father, and the power that makes man to have *koinōnía* (2842), partnership or participation in both the grace of the Lord Jesus Christ and the love of God the Father, is the Holy Spirit. Have you appropriated this marvelous and unmatched love and grace? If not, why delay any longer?

<u>LESSONS</u>:

1. The distinction must be made that the verbs *philéō*, to befriend, and *agapáō*, to love, and the nouns *philía* (5373), friendship, and *agápē* (26), divine love imparted by God, do not mean one and the same thing and should not be confused.

2. Paul is the only apostle who wrote, "my love," and is fully qualified through self-sacrifice to speak of the love of God in Christ as also his own love.
3. It was a love that did not discriminate as to whom it should be shown.
4. Whether the Corinthian believers agreed with Paul or not, the love which he expressed was not restricted in any way to his friends.
5. Paul uses the expression "Christ Jesus," and not "Jesus Christ," because he wanted to stress the deity of the Lord Jesus first.
6. It is God's will that each person should avail him or herself of His inexhaustible love and grace. If you have not, why not accept it now?

Bibliography

Blair, J. Allen. *Living Wisely.* Neptune, NJ: Loizeaux Brothers, 1973.

Fairbairn, Rev. Principal. "Three Kinds of Temptation." In *The Contemporary Pulpit* 10 (1888): 60, 61.

Hastings, James, ed. *The Great Texts of the Bible: 1 Corinthians.* London: The Waverly Book Co., Ltd., 1912.

Hastings, James, ed. *The Speaker's Bible: The First Epistle to the Corinthians* Vol. 2, *The Epistle to Philemon.* 208–221. Grand Rapids, MI: Baker Book House, 1962.

Ironside, H.A. *"Charge That to My Account" and Other Gospel Messages.* Chicago: Moody Press, 1931.

Jacob, John Alexander. *Building in Silence and Other Sermons.* London: Macmillan and Co., 1875.

Jowett, John Henry. *The Whole Armour of God.* Grand Rapids, MI: Baker Book House, 1969.

Liddon, H. P. *The Contemporary Pulpit Library Sermons.* London: Swan Sonnenschein & Co., 1892.

Maclaren, Alexander. *St. Paul's Epistles to the Corinthians.* New York: A.C. Armstrong and Son, 1910.

Moore, Aubrey L. *Some Aspects of Sin.* London: Percival & Co., 1891.

Morgan, G. Campbell. *The Corinthian Letters of Paul.* London: Oliphants Ltd., 1954.

Redpath, Alan. *The Royal Route to Heaven: Studies in First Corinthians.* Grand Rapids, MI: Fleming H. Revell, 1993.

Sadler, Rev. M. F. "Giving a Part of True Worship." In *The Churchman's Pulpit* 23 (1912): 75–77.

Selby, Thomas G. *The God of the Frail.* London: Hodder & Stoughton, 1902.

Simeon, Charles. *Expository Outlines on the Whole Bible.* Vol. 16. Grand Rapids, MI: Zondervan Publishing House, 1955.

Talmage, T. DeWitt. *500 Selected Sermons.* Grand Rapids, Michigan: Baker Book House, 1956.

Lexicons, Encyclopedias, and References for Greek Readers, from Classical and Koine Greek to Modern Greek

Byzantiou, S. D. *Lexikon tēs Hellēnikēs Glōssēs (Lexicon of the Hellenic Language).* Athens: Koromēla, A., 1852.

Dēmētrakou, D. *Lexikon tēs Hellēnikēs Glōssēs (Lexicon of the Hellenic Language).* Athens: Dēmētrakou, 1954.

Enkuklopaidikon Glōssologikon Lexikon (Encyclopedic Glossological Lexicon). Athens: Morfōtikē Hetaireia.

Enkuklopaidikon Lexikon Eleutheroudaki (Eleutheroudaki, Encyclopedic Lexicon). Athens: Eleutheroudakis, 1927.

Kalaraki, Michael and Nikolas Galanos. *Iōannou tou Chrusostomou Ta Hapanta (Complete Works of John Chrysostom)*, 1899.

Liddell, Henry George, and Robert Scott. *Greek–English Lexicon*, as Translated and Enriched by Xenophōn P. Moschos and Michael Kōnstantinides. Athens: John Sideris.

Megalē Helēnikē Enkuklopaideia (Great Hellenic Encyclopedia). Pursos (Pyrsos), Athens: Hēlios.

Neōteron Enkuklopaidikon Lexikon Hēliou (New Encyclopedic Lexicon "Hēlios"). Athens: Hēlios.

Papaoikonomou, George L. *Lexikon Anōmalōn Rhēmatōn (Lexicon of Irregular Verbs).* Athens: Kagiaphas.

Stamatakou, J. D., *Lexikon Archaias Hellēnikēs Glōssēs (Lexicon of the Ancient Hellenic Language).* Athens: Petrou Dēmētrakou, 1949.

Works by Spiros Zodhiates

A Richer Life for You in Christ. Chattanooga: AMG Publishers, 1972.

Editor, *The Complete Word Study Dictionary: New Testament.* Chattanooga: AMG Publishers, 1992.

Faith, Love, Hope. Chattanooga: AMG Publishers, 1985.

The Epistles of John. Chattanooga: AMG Publishers, 1994.

The Pursuit of Happiness. Chattanooga: AMG Publishers, 1987.

List of Abbreviations

acc. (accusative)

act. (active)

aor. (aorist [2 aor. for second aorist])

cf. (compare)

ch. (chapter)

comp. (composition)

dat. (dative)

etc. (and so forth)

ff. (following)

gen. (genitive)

i.e. (that is)

imperf. (imperfect)

indic. (indicative)

inf. (infinitive)

KJV (King James Version)

MT (Majority Text)

mid. (middle

n. d. (no date available)

N. p. (no publisher available)

NASB (New American Standard Bible)

NIV (New International Version)

NKJV (New King James Version)

nom. (nominative)

p. (page), pp. (pages)

part. (participle, participial)

pass. (passive)

perf. (perfect)

pl. (plural)

pres. (present)

pron. (pronoun)

Sept. (Septuagint)

sing. (singular)

TR (Textus Receptus)

UBS (United Bible Society)

usu. (usually)

v. (verse), vv. (verses)

vol. (volume)

Guide to the Transliteration and Modern Pronunciation of the Greek Alphabet

Capital Letter	Small Letter	Greek Name	Trans-literation	Phonetic Sound	Example
Α	α	alpha	*a*	a	as in father
Β	β	bēta	b	v	as in victory
Γ	γ	gamma	*g*	y	as in yell (soft guttural)
Δ	δ	delta	*d*	th	as in there
Ε	ε	epsilon	*e*	e	as in met
Ζ	ζ	zēta	*z*	z	as in zebra
Η	η	ēta	*ē*	ee	as in see
Θ	θ	thēta	*th*	th	as in thin
Ι	ι	iōta	*i*	i	as in machine
Κ	κ	kappa	*k*	k	as in kill (soft accent)
Λ	λ	lambda	*l*	l	as in land
Μ	μ	mē	*m*	m	as in mother
Ν	ν	nē	*n*	n	as in now
Ξ	ξ	xi	*x*	x	as in wax
Ο	ο	omicron	*o*	o	as in obey
Π	π	pi	*p*	p	as in pet (soft accent)
Ρ	ρ	ro	*r*	r	as in courage
Σ	σ,ς*	sigma	*s*	s	as in sit
Τ	τ	tau	*t*	t	as in tell (soft accent)
Υ	υ	ēpsilon	*u*	ee	as in see
Φ	φ	phi	*ph*	ph	as in graphic
Χ	χ	chi	*ch*	h	as in heel
Ψ	ψ	psi	*ps*	ps	as in ships
Ω	ω	omega	*ō*	o	as in obey

*At the end of words

SPECIAL RULES FOR THE TRANSLITERATION AND MODERN PRONUNCIATION OF THE GREEK LANGUAGE

COMBINATIONS OF CONSONANTS

Small Letter	Greek Names	Trans-literation	Phonetic Sound	Example
γγ	gamma + gamma	*gg*	g	as in go
γκ	gamma + kappa	*gk*	g	as in go
γχ	gamma + chi	*gch*	gh	as in ghost

DIPHTHONGS (DOUBLE VOWELS)

Small Letter	Greek Names	Trans-literation	Phonetic Sound	Example
αι	alpha + iōta	*ai*	ai	as in hair
αυ	alpha + ēpsilon	*au*	af, av	as in waft or lava
ει	epsilon + iōta	*ei*	ee	as in see
ευ	epsilon + ēpsilon	*eu*	ef, ev	as in effort or every
ηυ	ēta + ēpsilon	*ēu*	eef, eev	as in reef or sleeve
οι	omicron + iōta	*oi*	ee	as in see
ου	omicron + ēpsilon	*ou*	ou	as in group
υι	ēpsilon + iōta	*ui*	ee	as in see

BREATHINGS (Occur only with initial vowels)

(᾿) Smooth, not transliterated or pronounced.
When words begin with vowels, it may occur at the beginning of words with every vowel or double vowel (diphthong). ἔργον—*érgon*, work; εὐχή—*euchḗ*, vow.

(῾) Rough = h.
When words begin with vowels, it may occur at the beginning of words with every vowel or double vowel (diphthong). No distinction in pronunciation from the smooth breathing. To indicate the rough breathing we use "h" in the transliteration.

(ῥ) Rho = r.

(ὑ) Epsilon = u.
When these begin a word, they always have the rough breathing. There they are transliterated rh, hu, respectively. ῥέω—*rhéō*, flow; ὑπομονή—*hupomonḗ*, patience.

Scripture Index

Acts

Romans

1 Corinthians